Being Published

Patrick Semple

A Short Introduction
to Creative Writing

Code Green Publishing

ISBN 978-1-907215-21-6

Version 1.0

Cover design by Code Green Publishing

Published by
Code Green Publishing
Coventry, England

www.codegreenpublishing.com

Being Published

Also by Patrick Semple

A Parish Adult Education Handbook – Editor

Believe It Or Not – A Memoir

That Could Never Be – with K Dalton

The Rectory Dog – Poetry Collection

The Rector Who Wouldn't Pray For Rain – A Memoir

A Narrow Escape – Poetry Collection

Transient Beings – A Novel

Curious Cargo – A Travelogue

Acknowledgements

I would like to thank the following people and organisations:

Stonebridge Publishers for permission to quote from 'The Rectory Dog', 'A Narrow Escape' and 'Fine Books Made By Hand'.

Sarcone & Waeber for permission to quote Piet Hein's poem 'A poet should be ....'

John Banville for permission to quote from 'The Book of Evidence' and 'The Sea'.

Theo Dorgan for permission to quote from correspondence.

Michael Burrows for permission to quote from correspondence.

Code Green Publishing for permission to quote from correspondence.

Contents

Table of Contents

PREFACE

This book arose from my experience teaching the 'Creative Writing for Publication' course at the Adult and Community Education Department of The National University of Ireland, Maynooth.

Text books on any topic are important, but many aspects of practical application vary somewhat from theory. There is a place for both. My own experience of trying to be published was certainly different from my understanding of the theory of how the publishing world works.

I thought that it would be valuable for students to learn some of the realities that I encountered to put beside what they learned in their publishing classes. Part I is an account of my experience of dealing with publishers.

I have no doubt that a manuscript that is well written will influence a publisher positively over a manuscript that is not well written. Consequently I wrote Part II to highlight the main issues, as I see them, of writing good publishable English.

If, unlike Mrs Turkin in Chekhov's short story 'Ionych' whom you will encounter in the text, you hope to be published, I wish you well.

INTRODUCTION

There were nineteen adults aged from mid-twenties to mid-seventies, six men and thirteen women. They were a wonderfully diverse group of people. Amongst them a retired restaurateur, a young woman who worked with autistic children, a talented and accomplished artist, a retired nurse, a lecturer in mathematics, a cabinetmaker, a microbiologist, a psychotherapist and two young men, recent arts graduates both unemployed. This was a creative writing class at the Adult Education Department of the National University of Ireland, Maynooth. Some of them had declared themselves complete novices who wanted to discover if they had an aptitude to write creatively, while others had some experience of writing but mostly to do with their work. This was the second academic year that I had shared the teaching of this course of two semesters – from September to April. How I ended up as tutor in creative writing is still something of a mystery to me, but I will come to that.

In casual conversation during a coffee break one evening one of the students said to me: 'You should write another memoir.' I had already had two memoirs published. In declining the second one as a manuscript a friend of mine, a vastly experienced publisher of one of the largest publishing houses in Ireland, had told me that second memoirs are seldom successful and sell well below first memoirs by the same author. As it transpired my second memoir was published by a different publisher from the first one and sold every bit as well. Apart from the fact that I didn't have many memories that I hadn't already inflicted on the unsuspecting reader, I wouldn't want to tempt fate further by attempting a third. I explained this to those who were listening during our coffee break conversation.

'What I meant was,' the student said with a seriousness I interpreted as a device to reinforce the humour of her comment, 'a memoir of your previous life.' I laughed and said something to acknowledge her impishness and to share in her, to me, humorous comment. How wrong I was. She was deadly serious. Despite the fact that millions of people in the world believe in reincarnation I have always found it one of the craziest notions amongst many crazy notions that some religious people believe. Furthermore, even if I had had a former life and could remember anything of it I would probably not consider writing about it; I might have been a rabbit. Despite all of that, here I am starting something the first part of which might be called a literary memoir, if that is not too pretentious a term to use. It is about a facet of my recent life that I did not touch on in either of the first two memoirs: my efforts at being published and learning the craft of writing. I combine these two in the following pages. I now need to explain how I feel qualified to do so.

A novelist friend of mine, Suzanne Power, who had launched one of my books and knew my writing, approached me out of the blue to ask if I would share with her a creative writing course at Maynooth. She had already been sharing a similar course at the Maynooth extra-mural campus at Kilkenny with John MacKenna, another writer. They had been asked to provide the same course at the home campus, but John did not have time to take it on so I was asked if I would do it. I had had the experience of almost twenty years of my own writing, but needed to do some serious reading on the subject of creative writing. I worked hard at this over a full summer and subsequently with some trepidation I embarked on teaching my portion of the course, namely creative non-fiction and the short story. I gained confidence as time passed and I enjoyed the course immensely and by the time I had finished I had learned as much as I had taught. Then in teaching the second year, the class to which I referred above, I learned some more. I am now bold to share my experience of being published along with what I have learned about creative writing.

The

Industry

Chapter 1. Overview

My mother was a pedant. This was clear to me long before I knew the word. When I was a child she would correct not only my grammar and misuse of words, but she would also tut-tut at the use of slang that I had picked up at school, for slang was not used in my home. She was not a snob. She came from Cork and loved the idiom of the Cork 'shawlies' of the Coal Quay for whom she had an immense respect, and she appreciated Irish construction used in English, but when she used these it was clear that, despite the wonderful character of some of them, they were not Standard English.

When I went to boarding school, aged eleven, my education in written English began in earnest, not from my schoolmasters, but in my mother's replies to my letters home; spelling, punctuation, word use and layout. In my very first letter home I started, as I probably started most of my letters during my time at school: 'Dear Mum and Dad I recieved your letter......' I knew an ampersand would not have been acceptable, but I misspelled the word received as 'recieved.' The first point in the next letter from my mother was not about how I was settling in, what the school routine was or how I was finding new subjects, but **'i' before 'e' except after 'c,'**

so it is 'received'. As time went on I learned to avoid her censure by writing moderately correct English.

Those were the days, in the early 1950s, when children in primary school learned parsing and analysis. For those who have been taught English in school since parsing and analysis were abandoned, considered unnecessary as it was believed they were an inhibition to children's creativity, I give a brief account of what they involved.

To parse a sentence is to describe each word fully by naming it and to describe its function; a noun, a verb, a preposition, an adverb and so on. To analyse a sentence is to identify the form and function of words in it and to analyse its structure, for example to name the subject, verb, predicate, relative clause and so on. I have just looked up my dictionary to be sure I used 'predicate' correctly; it says; 'the word or words by which something is said about something.' Most un-dictionary like, 'something about something,' but clear none the less.

Given the content of the last two paragraphs it is not surprising that educationists (I have had to consult my dictionary again to see if it is 'educationalists' or 'educationists' to discover that either is acceptable. I have chosen 'educationists' because it sounds better to my ear) decided that parsing and analysis and all the grammar that used to be taught were an inhibition to creativity and that they should be discontinued in schools. I well remember trying to parse and analyse and detesting it and I have no doubt that it put off hundreds of thousands, if not, over the years, millions of children for life from any chance of developing a love of language. As in so many things the pendulum went from one extreme of its swing to the other and resulted in children not knowing the names or functions of parts of speech or understanding the structure of sentences and many of them learned to express themselves creatively in appalling English. My own adult interest in good English is the mature fruit of my mother's penchant for pedantry.

In the early 1960s all new entrants to Trinity College, University of Dublin, in their first term had to pass an essay in English on one of a choice of subjects written under exam conditions. An undergraduate who failed this essay twice was sent down. This essay exam was instituted because of the number of entrants highly qualified in other subjects who could not write proper English. Around the same time there was a controversy in the letters page of a national newspaper about newly qualified doctors who had graduated from University College, Dublin and who had written their applications for junior doctor posts to St Michael's Hospital Dun Laoghaire in very poor English. The problem has not gone away. Relatively recently a professor in a university scientific department, having read a draft of the thesis of an Irish PhD student, asked him sarcastically if English were his first language. I understand from a recently retired academic that if the Trinity essay were reintroduced today student numbers would be reduced considerably.

It needs to be said, however, that poor writing is not the exclusive preserve of Irish students. The most appallingly badly written book I have ever read was a biography of Shelley by an academic, published by Johns Hopkins University Press of that prestigious American University.

The poor writing of English amongst adults, even university students, led to the re-introduction into schools of the study of some grammar and syntax, the mid-way of the pendulum swing, but too late for some who even today are at a disadvantage when it comes to creative writing. If you fall into this category do not be discouraged, there are plenty of books from which, with a little application, you can learn in a short time what you need to know of these things.

The disappearance of Latin from the secondary curriculum of most schools was just as big a mistake as the removal of grammar from the primary schools. For pupils who were likely to become tradesmen, shop assistants or Wicklow sheep-farmers, I can understand not forcing them to learn Latin just for the sake of it. Not that a tradesman, shop assistant or a sheep-farmer might not benefit from studying Latin and might even become a writer in his spare time, but to deprive the more academic pupil of the opportunity to learn Latin was a tragedy.

Latin grammar gives a valuable grounding for learning the intricacies of English grammar and the grammar of other Romance languages such as French, Spanish and Italian. The nature of Latin grammar is such that it teaches logical thinking, reasoned choices and precision in the use of words. Since word order in Latin is different from that in English it gives insights and sensitivity in the structure of sentences. Furthermore Latin is the origin of many English words so that the study of the language enhances the student's English vocabulary.

Many of the advantages of learning Latin apply also to learning Greek. It is pushing it a bit far to expect the re-introduction of Latin and Greek into schools at a time when some universities are abolishing their classics departments.

Speaking of Greek, I want to take the opportunity to put in writing the following story told to me by an old classicist long since dead about Cork and Greek. Two elderly parish priests are walking along the Grand Parade in Cork deep in conversation. A newsboy keeping up beside them is pestering them to buy a copy of the evening paper 'The Echo.' Now a strong Cork accent adds an 'a' to Echo so the boy was shouting 'Echoa, Echoa.' The priests ignore him for a while but finally one of them in frustration turns to the newsboy and shouts back '*akēkoa, akēkoa*' which in Greek means 'I have heard, I have heard.'

Some acquaintance with Latin and Greek is a help. I was introduced to Latin in secondary school where those who taught it were hopeless teachers. In our first class in first form, without any preliminaries, we launched straight into learning by heart the present tense of first conjugation verbs '*amo, amas, amat...*' and we had to write it out a dozen times or be subjected to a scragging if we declined it wrongly. There was no introduction to the subject to say that Latin was the language of ancient Italy and of the Roman Empire, how it had become the language of educated Europe and

5

of the Church for centuries nor to discuss why it might be important to learn it. Thomas Jefferson wrote: 'To read Latin and Greek authors in their original is a sublime luxury.' I know a medical consultant whose great pleasure it is to read Latin and in his retirement plans to develop further his competence in the language. The method of teaching Latin to which I was subjected in school was to say nothing, explain nothing and beat the bare bones of it into children and put most of them off it for life.

Learning French was much the same. No introduction, no simple conversation to give confidence, no learning of a few phrases to appreciate the beautiful sound of the language before we launched into grammar. No; we went straight into learning by heart irregular verbs: *être, avoir* ... and irregular plurals: *hibou, caillou, bijou, chou* ..., and goodness knows what else to addle the brain and bore the wits out of most of us.

I learned Greek at university and could make some fist of it for a while, but lost most of it by not using it. One writer has said that '...Greek is a language of such breathtaking beauty and suppleness, and such expressive power that to read it is a kind of sensual pleasure.' I never advanced far enough in it to be able to confirm this! I learned a little Italian for use on annual visits to Tuscany, but could never hold a proper conversation; I retain only enough to book a table in a restaurant or buy a train ticket simply because between visits I don't use the little I have. Learning Irish was not such a torment to me as it was to many others since my primary school teacher had a love of the language and communicated something of that love to some of her pupils. In secondary school there was no conversation in Irish and it was taught by imposition and violence.

Let nobody feel that because they have only English they cannot start to write creatively or that they are handicapped in doing so. I tell you all of this to make the point that no matter how little knowledge you may have of other languages the little you have can enhance your use of English and the pleasure of writing, for language is the stock-in-trade of the creative writer.

Our English master was at the other end of the spectrum from those who taught Latin, French and Irish in secondary school. At the beginning of class, without a word of introduction, he would launch into a theatrical reading of a couple of pages of a novel that had caught his fancy; *Don Camillo* was one I remember, or a few stanzas of a poem; the *Rubáiyát* was a favourite of his. After his performance, and performance it was, he would say a few words about what he had just read, bang the book closed and proceed with the subject of the day. I have no doubt that some of the class thought he was crazy, but even the quality of life of a Wicklow sheep-farmer would be enhanced if while dipping or shearing his sheep he were able to recite to himself a few stanzas of the *Rubáiyát of Omar Khayyám*. After all many a poet and writer was brought up on a farm including Virgil who wrote extensively about agriculture.

A surprising number of people are illiterate. In Ireland the figure for those who cannot read or write at all is approximately seven per cent. A further close to twenty-three per cent of the population is only functionally literate; that is to say they can read words like 'Stop', 'Danger', 'Exit', the names of the runners on the racing page of newspapers, if that's their interest, and little more. So, approximately thirty percent of the population is illiterate. They cannot understand foreign films with subtitles and they cannot read more than the simplest public notices, and communication in society for them is very difficult.

Many people who are perfectly literate have little occasion to write in their family or social life or in their work. Like any skill that is not used it becomes rusty and facility in it diminishes. Such people become less comfortable writing. The work other people do means that they write a good deal within a limited area, for example clerks and officials of all kinds and some people in their work write reports, often long and complex: for example social workers, lawyers and researchers. Many of these people are extremely fluent and articulate, but none of this writing is what is called creative writing and many of them may not have the aptitude to write creatively.

At an event in The Writers' Centre, Dublin, the Northern Ireland writer Sam McAughtry, referring to writers in his speech before announcing the winner of a short story competition said: 'You can either write or you can't.' He himself left school at 14, served in the Royal Air Force during the war and subsequently worked as a labourer and civil servant before becoming a full-time writer. He made his point simply without developing it. What I think he meant was that the person who hasn't the facility to write cannot be taught to write creatively. Without an aptitude to write you cannot become a writer. Such a person can learn the ways and techniques of writing but will never be a writer in the same way that a person without the ability to draw will never be an artist or a person who hasn't an ear for music will never be a musician. However, although I have ended up writing late in life, I would never call myself a writer any more than I would call myself a poet because I write poetry. In reply to T.S.Eliot's question to him as to what he wanted to do, Stephen Spender said 'Be a poet.' Eliot responded: 'I can understand you wanting to write poems, but I don't quite know what you mean by "being a poet".' Writers are people who make a significant part of their living by writing. There is only a tiny number of these in any community and with few exceptions writers have a second string to their bow; more often than not, teaching or lecturing.

What then is creative writing? It can be fiction, non-fiction or poetry. It is not academic or professional writing, journalism, comment or reporting. Creative writing says something about the human condition by using language that is pleasurable to read. Creative writing contributes to the content and enhances the experience of reading. It says something about being human and explores the mystery that surrounds us. It ranges from popular romance that deals in the universal but mysterious phenomenon of falling in love and the whole world of romance in all its complexity to the work of some of the world's great writers who in their novels plumb philosophically the depths of the human condition.

Creative non-fiction is writing such as memoir, essay, travel writing, food writing or writing about nature. The word 'creative' refers to the use of language that enhances the experience of reading. Non-fiction is factual and accurate writing about real people, places and events and uses creative language in portraying them. The writer of creative non-fiction does not invent or make up things. They make ideas and facts interesting by their mode of expression and the language they use.

Fiction in literature is about the truth of some aspect of being human using the novel, the short story, poetry and drama. It is the invention of characters, settings and events that convey truth about aspects of life and living. Fairy tales are fiction, they have never happened but they convey truths about how real people behave. There are fairy godmothers, ugly sisters and Cinderellas in real life. Fiction writers don't copy real people and neither do they invent people completely. They use bits of real people; they base their characters on parts of actual characters. They use small detail from real lives. They also base settings on real places and events on real happenings.

Now I am jumping ahead as I deal more fully with these topics in Part 2 – Chapter 3, and I want to return to how I started to write.

Chapter 2. Beginner's Luck

In 1987, aged forty eight, I was Adult Education Officer on the staff of the Church of Ireland Theological College. As I sat in my office one afternoon the telephone rang. It was the Church's press officer. She told me she had arranged a course for diocesan press officers at the School of Journalism, Rathmines, to help them with preparing copy to submit to editors of diocesan magazines. She recounted that there were three or four places on the course that had not been taken up, and she asked me to fill one to help to make up the numbers. Though it was not in my field of interest, on the principle that knowledge is no burden, I accepted. It was a day long course that David Rice the head of the School taught. I enjoyed it and, amongst other things I have since forgotten, I learned about pyramids in writing journalistic reports and how people read newspapers. It had been a day well spent.

About a month later a funny thing happened that as far as I was aware had nothing to do with the course. One day I went back to my office after lunch, sat down at my desk and wrote a short story. It was fiction but it was based upon an unlikely couple that I had known who lived in a remote place up the hills in the heart of the country. I called it *Bill's Wife*. At that time I knew absolutely nothing about writing short stories or about creative writing. I just wrote the story and went over it a few times to make changes, correct the English and make it as readable as possible. Then the question was what to do with it. I might easily have put it into a drawer, forgotten it and would probably have thrown it out when I was leaving that job. I remembered David Rice who had been so good on the course which he had ended generously by saying that if he could help us in any way not to hesitate to contact him. It being the days before PCs I had written the story longhand, so I asked the College secretary if she would type it out for me and I sent it to David. I asked him to be totally honest and not to hesitate to tell me if it was rubbish.

David replied quickly and said simply; 'This is an ideal story for *Ireland's Own*, send it to them.' I did as he suggested, got on with my life and forgot all about it. Four or five months later I was on holiday in the small village of Stratford-on-Slaney, in Co Wicklow. One morning I was walking up to the village to the shop when a friend put her head out her window and said:

'I've just read your story.'

'What story?' I asked.

'In *Ireland's Own*.'

As they say using that lovely Irish construction: I nearly fell out of my standing. I tried not to look surprised, said something vague and continued on my way, walking on air. On reflection, however, I was not entirely convinced because I had heard nothing from *Ireland's Own* since I had sent the story to them. Surely if they were going to publish it they would have let me know. I would not be sure that it had been published until I saw it with my own eyes in black and white.

When I arrived at the shop I asked if they had a copy of *Ireland's Own*. They hadn't. On the way back I called to my friend and asked if I might borrow her copy. When I arrived home I opened the paper and there it was: *A Short Story by Patrick Semple; Bill's Wife*, with a poor and inappropriate line drawing illustration. I read the story and I was ten feet tall.

A few days later I told a friend who knew something about writing and publishing about *Bill's Wife*. His first comment was: 'Make sure they pay you.' I had not even thought about payment. In fact when he said it I thought it vulgar and mercenary to think about money in the context of my major contribution to world literature! I knew what Dr Johnson had said: 'No man but a blockhead ever wrote except for money.' I already had a job and thought no more about what my friend had said. Some weeks later I met him again.

'Did that crowd pay you for your story?'

'No.' I said.

'Well, get on to them. They're part of the 'Independent Group' and the fee is as good to you as it is to Tony O'Reilly. If your story is good enough for them to publish it's good enough for them to pay you.'

I phoned the *Ireland's Own* office and spoke to a man who said in an offhand way that he'd look into it. A month or so later there was no word, so I phoned again. In about a week I received a cheque for £10. My great regret today is that I didn't frame it, but £10 came in handy at the time to an impecunious cleric.

Needless to say this encouraged me. I oscillated between 'this is easy' on the one hand and '*Bill's Wife* was a flash in the pan' on the other. The truth transpired, as it often does, to be somewhere between the two. I had read Frank O'Connor short stories when I was younger. My mother remembered him as a child in Cork. He lived up Summerhill beyond her home in St Luke's. She remembers young Michael O'Donovan, as he was then, as a schoolboy passing her house on his way to or from the library with a pile of books under his arm. He always seemed to be on his own. James Plunkett said of Frank O'Connor that most of his literary work came from his childhood and early youth. He referred to those periods of life as containing the store of material which is all a good writer can draw on. Flannery O'Connor (not related), the American short story writer, said that anyone who survived childhood knows enough about life to last them the rest of their days.

Louis Auchinloss said:

'Childhood is the writer's only capital.'

I came across all of this consensus many years after *Bill's Wife* was published and understood them to refer to something we know: that it is during childhood the mind soaks in like blotting-paper, in a way that it doesn't do later in life, all that it has the potential to absorb. Much of this knowledge, awareness and intuition is stored in the subconscious and the unconscious and it is from that store that the writer draws in later life the material that informs his or her writing.

Almost without knowing how, I had written a short story that worked. The question then arose: how do I begin to write another?

Simone de Beauvoir has recounted that after a book of hers had been published successfully she started her next book with the same trepidation and uncertainty as she had begun the previous one. In other words one success does not guarantee another which is the substance of an aphorism one often hears: 'a writer is only as good as his last book.'

Since I really didn't know how *Bill's Wife* had happened I wasn't sure how to start again. I had written it without any knowledge of the theory of short stories, their structure or essential characteristics. All I knew was that I should write in good English, employing all that I needed to know from the tedium of parsing and analysis, paragraphing, punctuation and spelling, keep it short and make every word count. Encouraged by my beginner's luck, ideas for stories started to come that were indeed mostly suggested by characters, settings and events from my childhood.

By now I had my first computer; an Amstrad without a mouse. It took me ages to teach myself how to use it. After a while I had the hang of it and it made writing so much easier. First of all I didn't have to be careful to write legibly so that I could read what I had written when I went back over the story. Secondly it was easy to cut and paste sentences and paragraphs to improve the ordering of the narrative and whereas it didn't draw my attention to split infinitives and dangling prepositions, it did enable me to check my spelling.

I started many a story and scrapped it when I had an idea of the characters and maybe the setting but I hadn't worked out before I started exactly where the story was going. After about two years when I had half a dozen or so completed stories I noticed in the RTE Guide a quarter hour short story programme on Radio 1. I phoned the station and asked for information. They sent me details that included the requirement that the story should be close to 950 words. I picked four stories and had to edit them all down to as close as possible to a 950 word count. I learned a great deal from having to decide what to omit. In all cases what I left out improved the story. In fact I have no doubt that over the years I have never reduced a story to fit a required word count that it did not make it a better short story. It is easy to be verbose. The short story writer must learn not to include anything that does not contribute to moving the narrative forward and to make every word count.

To my great delight the producer selected one of the stories for broadcast and returned the others. This was two and a half years after the publication of *Bill's Wife*. RTE could not have been in greater contrast to *Ireland's Own*; they were businesslike. They sent a printed letter with individual particulars inserted telling me that a provisional booking had been made, and asking my permission to broadcast, giving name of story, time and date of broadcast and stating a fee of £60.

I signed the blue form they had attached and had it in the post on the evening I received it before somebody changed their mind. £60 was a fortune to me for the satisfaction of writing a story; however I remembered Dr Johnson and decided I would accept the fee!

The story was about a man who delivered newspapers. The idea came from a real newspaperman in the town of my childhood that I combined with aspects of another newspaperman I had known in my adolescence. An entirely fictitious story but the main character came from characteristics of two people in real life. I told a couple of close friends about the broadcast and couldn't wait to hear it myself. By now I was living in the country and had a meeting at 8.00 pm about five miles away from home on the evening *Doc* was going out on air. I listened to it in the car and when I arrived at the meeting venue I sat on in the car to hear it to the end. A professional actor read the story and in my opinion he didn't read it very well. Some of his emphases were wrong; he sometimes laid stress on nouns rather than verbs. None the less I was pleased, but was disappointed that when I entered the room for the meeting the assembled company did not stand up and applaud, despite not having heard it. At the end of the meeting a man who had come in late asked me: 'Was that your story on the radio tonight?' I said that it was, but he moved on without saying another word. He didn't say that he liked it nor did he make a comment to say he didn't know I did that kind of thing.

About four months after the broadcast I received a letter from Maxwell Sweeney the producer of the programme asking me if I would send him *Arthur and Jess*, one of the stories he had not used first time round. The idea for it came to me from a couple who were friends of my parents when I was a child, both long since dead leaving no relations that I knew of, so I had no difficulty with Arthur in the story having an affair which my parents' friend was most unlikely to have had. No matter how you mask a character there will always be somebody to find themselves in your fiction and take offence. Iris Murdoch confessed to having terrible trouble with this but denied everything to her friends and accused them of vanity when they thought they recognised themselves in her novels.

About six months later Maxwell Sweeney broadcast another of my short stories, *Home*, about a man who worked in finance in London and came home to farm when his father died and in doing so made the mistake of his life until he fell in love with a Dutch woman who ran a market garden nearby. Though not churchgoers they took in the local clergyman who had AIDS and were prepared to look after him until he died.

Over the years I had written poems from time to time. Shortly after the broadcast of *Home* I became bolder (in the English, not in the Irish, sense) and sent a collection of my poems to *The Blackstaff Press* in Belfast. In time they declined them but while doing so they asked me if I had any short stories. I wondered if they had been listening secretly to RTE Radio 1. I sent them a number of what I considered my best stories and they selected one for inclusion in

The Second Blackstaff Book of Short Stories planned for publication later that year. The story, *The Pass*, is about a birdwatcher, a species, if you'll excuse the pun, considered by many people to be a bit 'wallyish', like vegetarians. I was a birdwatcher for many years and have been a vegetarian for 27 years. I also wear socks with my sandals!

My experience of *Blackstaff*, as with RTE, could not have been in greater contrast from my experience of *Ireland's Own*. *Blackstaff* were professional. They told me early on that they were going to use one of my stories and in time they sent me proofs to read and correct. They pointed out a few bits and pieces they suggested that I change. Most of their suggestions were good and I agreed. One or two I didn't agree with and had a conversation of about half an hour on the phone about these with an editor trying to reach a compromise on the use of a word or two and the structure of a sentence. Needless to say the editor was wrong!

Chapter 3. The Memoirs

I was born into a Church of Ireland family in 1939 in Wexford Town and spent my childhood there. Those were the days of Catholic triumphalism when very little if anything stirred in the country, including the government, without the approval of the Catholic Hierarchy. By the year 2000 there had been Vatican II, television, improved education, travel and other things that meant the loosening of the rigid control of the Catholic Church over Irish society. Ecumenism was the order of the day and Protestants were looked on by the vast majority of Catholics less as heretics than as just different. In those days I had had many conversations about religion with Catholic friends including clergy and realised that Catholics generally had little idea, not surprisingly, what it was like to have been brought up Protestant. In fact Catholics had many misconceptions about Protestants. I was interested in this kind of issue and decided I would try to write a memoir recounting from the inside what it was like to have been born into and to have lived in the tiny, less than 5%, Protestant minority, stretching from those early days of Catholic hegemony to the more ecumenical and liberal society that was Ireland at the beginning of the third millennium.

Different people write at different times of the day. By temperament, or even genetically, some are morning people and get up early and write when rested and fresh. Others are night-time people who only begin to write at eleven o'clock at night when everybody else in the house has gone to bed and then work through to the small hours. I had no difficulty deciding when I should write; I am a lark and decidedly not an owl.

When I started to write the memoir I was living in Monkstown and working in the north inner city. My computer was on a desk in the corner of the bedroom and every morning at 6.00am, careful not to waken my wife, I would write for up to two hours before getting ready to go to work. I would get out of bed, put on my dressing-gown, cross the room and sit straight down at the computer. If I as much as went downstairs to make a cup of tea, I was likely to distract myself and not write at all. I found that I had to be disciplined in this way or some excuse for not writing would present itself to me. Writing is hard work and a lonely pursuit and it is easier not to write than to write. Recently I came across this quote of an American poet, Gwendolyn Brooks: 'Art hurts. Art urges voyages – and it is easier to stay at home.' One morning I sat in front of the computer and nothing would come. I told myself that I was wasting my time and nobody would be interested anyway and nobody would want to publish it. I turned off the computer and went back to bed. After about ten minutes while I was lying there awake it came to me that if I didn't write this memoir nobody else would. I went back to the computer and started to write, and although there were other blips from time to time after many early mornings I finally finished it.

It is standard and good advice to people who write not to ask your spouse or other member of your family to give an opinion on something you have written. They may find it difficult to be objective; they may be deferentially uncritical or they may be over critical. Neither is helpful. In either case, in fact no matter what they say their comments may interfere with the equilibrium of a marriage or family relationship.

Hilary, my wife, taught English in her early days and is a wonderful copy-editor and proof-reader. She read the final work, and in order to preserve our marriage, she was under strict instructions not to comment on content. She corrected spelling, capitals, paragraphing and everything else except content until we had a presentable manuscript. These days most publishers want a submission that is as close as possible to being finished. Copy-editing takes time and, as time is money, this can militate against the decision to accept a manuscript for publication. If a publisher saw in you a second James Joyce or J K Rowling they would probably accept a submission in any condition from you and work it into publishable form, but if you are a struggling nonentity you help your cause by presenting a final manuscript in good condition, needing as little copy-editing as possible.

The next question is: to whom should I submit the memoir? Conventional wisdom is that an author should choose a publisher who specialises in the genre into which the work fits. There is no point in submitting an adult literary novel to a publisher who specialises in children's literature or a book about mountain climbing or flying to one who specialises in maritime publications. Needless to say while I was writing I had a particular publisher in mind. Columba Press was a successful publisher of religious work of all kinds and since I had spent most of my adult life in the ministry of the Church of Ireland I submitted the manuscript to them. In about six or eight weeks, which is a short period for a decision, I had a telephone call from the publisher to say he would like to publish and could we meet for lunch to discuss it? I was ecstatic; a proper book between two covers, albeit paper ones, that would have my name on it. We met for lunch and he fulfilled the expectation I had from friends who knew him as a kindly affable man. We had a most agreeable lunch during which he informed me that the book would sell for €12.99 and that I would receive 10%. When later I recounted to a publisher friend that my royalties would be 10%, his immediate response was: '10% of what?' I naively assumed it was 10% of €12.99, but it transpired that it was 10% of the discounted price to the bookshops or distributors.

There were three things in the manuscript the publisher suggested I consider omitting. One was a detail that might allow a reputed paedophile schoolmaster, though dead, to be identified, which could be unfair to his family. When he pointed out the possibility that this might happen, I readily agreed to leave the detail out. I would have been appalled if anything I had said might have meant the man could have been identified on hearsay evidence.

The second was a reference to an Englishman whose name was Handcock. So integrated into Irish society had he become that some smart alec suggested he should use the Irish version of his name. 'And what would that be?' he had asked. 'Manus O'Toole,' came the reply. I agreed to omit this too, as it seemed to offend the publisher's sensibilities. It was more likely that as a mainly religious publisher, it was the sensibilities of his religious book buyers that concerned him.

The third was a critical implication in which I had referred to the fact that Archbishop Robin Eames was chairman of the Council which abolished the Adult Education Council of the Church of Ireland. He had written not long previously a preface to an Adult Education Handbook saying that 'it is impossible to overestimate the importance of Adult Education for the Church.' I agreed to omit the reference, though convinced that Robin, whom I knew personally, was made of sterner stuff than to allow this to offend him. He was far more likely to say: 'One up for you, Pat.' During the lunch some reference was made to a launch of my memoir in due course. The publisher played down the possibility by saying: 'A launch is just a night out for an author.' It was clear that he wanted to discourage the idea.

Conscious that 'there's many a slip 'twixt cup and lip,' only when the proofs arrived to be corrected was I finally convinced that the book would be published. At this stage I was dealing primarily with

Brian, the publisher's promotions manager, who never mentioned any reservation about a launch. I took it for granted that there would be one and, on the suggestion of a friend, I asked him if we could have it in Wexford where the story began. Wexford featured prominently in the early chapters and it was likely to be of particular local interest there. He agreed. I can perfectly understand that as a businessman a publisher must measure the value of the publicity of a launch and the sales that are made at it against the cost of it.

I met people at the launch of *Believe It Or Not* that I hadn't met since my childhood fifty years previously and there was great positive publicity in the local press. The launch was followed, as is expected of authors, by time spent working with Brian to promote sales. As is the practice of publishers he sought as much publicity for the book in the media as possible. As is also standard practice he sent out review copies to newspapers and radio stations of all kinds, national and local, exploiting all of his media contacts. The one I remember most clearly was an interview on Marian Finucane's prime time morning show on RTE Radio 1. She gave the book very good exposure and I particularly remember two things from the interview. The first was her amusement at my mentioning the effect on the gait of my primary school teacher of her martyrdom to corns. The other was Marian saying how she had always felt sorry for Protestants who as children had to attend Sunday school. The book was very well received and in particular local newspapers around the country where I had been in parishes gave it good publicity with articles and photographs.

The Arts Council of Ireland paid my fare, and Hilary and I went to Australia, Melbourne and Sydney, to promote the memoir. In Melbourne the publisher's agent was a delightful woman, Marie, who arranged a successful launch where I met a fascinating cross-section of Irish Australians. We had the opportunity to see some friends near Melbourne and Marie invited us to a barbecue at her home on the Sunday that we were there. Sydney was a different story. There I had the distinction of an experience that I had read of, recounted by some renowned authors, of having a book launch to which nobody came. We waited over an hour and then went home. The Australian agent's man in Sydney hadn't done his homework. During the evening as we sat chatting, waiting in vain for people to arrive, he confided in us perfectly seriously that one day he intended to be Prime Minister of Australia!

We also went to Canada, with the help of the Arts Council, to promote the book in Toronto. There the publisher's agent was a taciturn individual but he did his work well. He arranged for me to be interviewed by some radio and television programmes. One of these was a radio interview with Colm O'Brien from County Cavan, who with his wife Betty brought us out for a day to show us the environs of Toronto and then to their home for a meal. The highlight of the visit was an invitation for me to address a Toronto – Ireland Chamber of Commerce lunch. After the book signing I was shown to a table. A man already sitting there stood up, put out his hand and said: 'My name's Pat Quinn.' I recognised him from his round open face, his trade mark white polo neck shirt and his low stature. He was the one-time supermarket king of Ireland who ran into trouble with a leisure centre, including a famous rope ski slope, in Kilternan. He went to Toronto where he had two very successful Irish bar/restaurants. When I spoke, my account of the book and why I had written it were well received. Most of those present were aware that things in Ireland had moved on, but many of them had left the country at a time when ecumenism here was unknown. After the lunch eight or ten of us decamped to one of Pat Quinn's bars and had a pleasant afternoon.

While all the foregoing preparation, publication and promotion was going on I had already started another book. A friend of mine, Kevin Dalton, who was Rector of Monkstown, had had a far more interesting life than mine. One day I said to him:

'Why don't you write your story?'

'Why,' he said, 'who'd be interested?'

After a lot of persuasion he finally said:

'OK, I'll tell you what I'll do. I'll tell it if you'll write it.'

I first met Kevin in a pub one afternoon after rugby in 1958 and bumped into him on and off at Saturday night parties and 'hops' over a period of a year or so. Without knowing it both of us were considering ordination. We became friendly and Kevin told me his story. I summarise it here largely as I did for the blurb I wrote for the book.

Kevin spent his life from 1934 when he was two until he was sixteen in orphanages. His story is a remarkable victory of spirit over adversity. From an early age he wanted to be ordained and this ambition waxed and waned through all the vicissitudes of early disadvantage. He arrived in Dublin aged eighteen with only a primary education and without a job. This was 1951 when there were few jobs to be had. Unemployment was endemic and thousands of people were emigrating to find work. He pounded the footpaths of Dublin calling to shops and businesses looking for work. He hid his torn trousers and scruffy clothes under a long overcoat. After two months without success he was demoralised and considered going to England.

He eventually found work in Dublin and subsequently qualified as a miller, but still had to confront his lifelong ambition to be ordained. While working during the day he set about studying for university entrance. After much effort he eventually passed and entered Trinity in 1961. In 1966 he was ordained in the Church of Ireland and spent a year of postgraduate study in America. His ministry was spent in parishes in Dublin.

In an orphanage in Limerick he was often hungry, but on a farm in Co Tipperary where he worked before he came to Dublin he was 'as happy as Larry.' His story is one of pathos and humour. His life was one of determination to survive and to achieve an ambition against the odds.

The plan was that Kevin would record his material onto tape, his secretary would type it up and I would use the transcripts to write his story. At first he didn't take the project seriously and it was difficult to persuade him to produce the tapes. When he did he was usually in a hurry and didn't speak clearly so that the transcripts in places were incomprehensible. When I pointed this out to him his response was along the lines: 'It's all right for you, you've nothing else to do. I've a parish to run. Who's going to be interested anyway?'

Eventually I put a first draft together and showed it to Columba who said they would publish it. Kevin then began to take it marginally more seriously. He was still hard to tie down and on one occasion when he arrived with a chapter I had given him to read, so uncooperative was he that I was tempted to fire him out and the rest of the manuscript after him. Despite everything I finally finished it and Kevin chose the title *That Could Never Be.*

After Kevin had left the orphanage in Limerick and was working on a farm near Thurles, Co Tipperary he had come to know Des Hanafin, of the well-known political family. When it was time for the launch Kevin asked Mary, Des's daughter, who at the time was a government minister, to be guest speaker. Mary volunteered the venue, a conference room in Government buildings. When replies to the invitations began to come in it became obvious that the room that held about 150 people would not be big enough. It was transferred to City Hall where approximately 300 people attended a highly successful launch. The memoir sold very well. It did as I had predicted to Kevin when trying to encourage him to take it seriously: it sold better than mine.

One film producer showed an interest in the story but nothing came of it.

Chapter 4. Success and Rejection

During the time I was writing *That Could Never Be* I had sent a short story, *Ted*, in five instalments, an episode a day Monday to Friday, to Lyric FM classical music radio station as a submission to their *Quiet Quarter* slot. I made the mistake that no writer should make: I hadn't done my research to discover that what they broadcast in *Quiet Quarter* was not short stories but non-fiction. Despite this I had a call from the producer Eithne Tinney to say she would use it. Eithne was a woman with a mind of her own who subsequently famously had herself elected to the board of a building society as a protest member representing ordinary depositors and became a thorn in the flesh of the society's board of suits.

I once sent Theo Dorgan a copy of a poetry collection of mine that was published, which I will come to later. I had an encouraging letter back from him the last paragraph of which read:

'I wish the book well, and hope it brings you back unexpected messages from the world: that's the thing about books, I find, you set them off on the stream and you never know where they'll end up.'

That's exactly what happened with the short story *Ted* on *Quiet Quarter*. Shortly after the last instalment had been broadcast I received a letter, redirected to me by Lyric FM, from a German couple who had heard the story in their holiday cottage in Donegal.

Horst and Linde Altstetter were retired schoolteachers from near Kempten in Bavaria, a town that is twinned with Sligo. They both taught English to adult groups at home and asked if I would let them have a copy of *Ted*, which had a Christmas theme, to use with their groups approaching Christmas. I was flattered to be asked, thanked them and sent them a copy of the story.

Some time later I started to receive letters from individual members of the groups in Bavaria. I soon became confused as to which group each of them belonged. I wrote to Horst and Linde for clarification and for my own purposes named the three groups as follows: *The Hard Tickets* because I had had a hilarious letter from them introducing themselves as a group of eight women that Horst taught. They said that originally there had been a couple of men in the group but they had kicked them out. They wanted to know why I had ended the story as I had, and 'why you didn't let Ted come home for Christmas.' Naturally I replied that I hadn't stopped him. The second group, that Linde taught I called *The Wrinklies* as they were a group of older people and the third was the *Sligo/Kempten Group*.

The following summer Horst and Linde invited Hilary and me to meet them in Donegal. We stayed with friends nearby and spent a most congenial day together. They invited us to Kempten for a week where we met the groups and where they had arranged for me to do some readings; one a public reading in the town, another to a large group of teachers and readings to the senior English classes of two schools. We received the warmest of hospitality; we were invited to the homes of members of the groups and taken for day outings when we were free. One of these was to Oberammergau near the border with Austria. We arrived home after a wonderful week exhausted and ready for a holiday. We have been twice since to Kempten on similar trips all as the result of Eithne Tinney taking a chance on a short story rather than non-fiction, and as Theo Dorgan said about books: 'You set them off on a stream and you never know where they'll end up.' The world of writing is a world of networking and chance.

When you write a short story the question is what to do with it. Publishers notoriously shy away from or often say an unequivocal 'no thank you' to short story collections because they are not a business proposition; they sell badly, although you frequently meet people who tell you they love short stories, especially travelling or on holiday as they can finish one in a short time at an airport or on a plane or between swims on a beach. Of course collections of the great short story masters of the past, Anton Chekhov, Guy de Maupassant and the Irish master of the genre, Frank O'Connor, all sell well. So do the collections of writers like for example H.H. Munro (Saki) and of course the contemporary Irish master, William Trevor. Publishers won't give a second thought to collections from unknown or barely-known authors.

So what does a literary nonentity do with his short stories except put them into a drawer and forget them in the hope that their children or grandchildren may find them when the literary nonentity is dead and gone, and discover that their parent or grandparent was after all an unacknowledged literary genius? There are outlets for individual short stories: commercial magazines, literary reviews, anthologies and above all short story competitions. For magazines you need to buy a few editions and discover the kind and length of story they publish. For competitions you need to find out the rules and stick strictly to them.

You can spend a fair proportion of your time sending stories to any or all of these and may I suggest that if you do, that you keep a little book and enter, with date, what you have sent to whom. Over the years I did not do this and sent many stories to magazines or radio that disappeared into the ether and were never heard of again. Not that I expected them to be returned, or a competition organiser to tell me that I hadn't been successful. I would, however, expect a publisher to do so, but more often than not they don't.

Once, by mistake, I sent a story to the doyen of judges of the Irish short story and compiler of anthologies, Louis Marcus, that I had sent to him some considerable time before for consideration for a previous competition or anthology. He returned it to me with an impertinent note telling me I had sent this story to him once before, and not to send it to him again. Wow!

I never won a competition and eventually became fed up sending away stories to them. I comfort myself by something my mother used to say when I was a child. When she was young she bred wire-haired fox terriers and entered them for shows: 'Who wins,' she used to say, 'depends on who judges.' On the other hand I'm prepared to accept that it's perfectly possible that my stories were simply not good enough.

One day I had a phone call from a man who told me he was a printer and asked me if I could let him have an electronic copy of my story.

'What story?' I asked.

'I'm printing the *Cork Literary Review*.'

I had sent a story to the editor of the Review, some months before and just like *Bill's Wife* and *Ireland's Own*, since I didn't keep a little book to record what I sent away I had forgotten all about it.

'Are you sure?' I asked. 'What's the name of the story?'

'*Dinner Out.*'

I remembered. I sent him a disc of the story and phoned the Review office to confirm. The person who answered the phone wouldn't tell me if the story would be in the Review or not. I became suspicious of what was going on. About half an hour later a senior person phoned me and confirmed that my story would be used and apologised that the first person would not confirm it. The explanation was simple: the result of a poetry competition was to be announced in the next edition and staff members were warned not to give any information over the phone. A conscientious junior extended the order to cover short stories as well.

When I went to the launch of the *Cork Literary Review* I was amused, but not the slightest put out, that the editor or anybody else did not speak to me at all. Afterwards Hilary and I and a few friends who had come with us had a wonderful meal and night out in Cork's famous vegetarian restaurant, arguably the best vegetarian restaurant in Ireland. Writing and being published are not the only pleasures in life.

There is nothing more daunting, especially for a person who has recently started to write, than to sit down and be faced with a blank page, though these days it is almost always a blank screen, to discover that nothing will come. All kinds of excuses arise in the mind: 'people who write are all more able than I am'; 'I really don't know enough about this'; 'I'd be better off to paint the back kitchen;' 'wanting to become a writer is just a fantasy'. Stop that! The very fact that you have started means there is some motivation and facility there to write. If nothing will come, write anything, literally anything; what you did yesterday, how you felt on your first visit to the zoo; how you feel about going to the dentist, how you developed an interest in something you know you do well. When you have written for about half an hour just leave it there, don't even read over it, and do the same thing tomorrow, and the next day until you are in the habit and by then something of value to write about will present itself to you. Whatever you do, don't give up. When I was a student, an academic who was a writer read an essay I had written. When he had commented on the content he said; 'You should write a little every day.' That's all he said. I didn't know what he was talking about. Many years later I remembered what he had said and I believe he saw that I had some facility to write and wanted to encourage me. If he had been more explicit I might have started writing earlier in life, or I might not as in those days I was busy saving the world.

Two of the most important things that a writer must learn to accept and learn from are criticism and rejection. A completed piece of work is just like one's own child: it may not be perfect but don't point out to me the imperfections. Tell me about the good bits. Writers need to be prepared to accept constructive criticism of their work. In fact they should seek it out and welcome it as the only way to improve and to maintain a high standard. A cousin of mine in England is a full-time writer. He submits nothing to his agent without first asking a writer friend to read it and taking account of his criticism.

Traditionally there are two categories of criticism, destructive and constructive. I once read a critique of a novel in a newspaper by a writer I know. His book had been generally well received but this critic had used the opportunity for some reason to devastate the book and launch an *ad hominem* attack on the author. In the *Review* section of the *Irish Times* another reviewer, who shall be nameless, batters by invective a poor unfortunate novelist who had the effrontery to publish a second novel that she considers was not up to the standard of his first. She proceeds to launch a vicious attack on it. She went so far as to say something to the effect that he could have held his head up if he had stopped after the first and not written the second at all. Of course his second novel may not have been in the same class as his first, but the critic could have said so without the venom that she used. Her criticism said more about her than it did about the book.

Our over-sensitivity to criticism, even constructive criticism, can come from childhood vulnerabilities that are part of the adult person we are. Some of these childhood vulnerabilities are so deep that we are not aware of them, and some are immediately brought to the surface by a word or phrase from childhood that a critic uses. Writers must cultivate the capacity to accept genuine criticism and learn from it. It is sometimes not easy, but it may be a key to something with which we have been subconsciously ill at ease. We should be able to identify destructive criticism and learn to put it aside. It can be painful and if we allow it to it will cripple us. When we are criticised we should remind ourselves of something creative we have done successfully in the past to affirm our confidence and keep writing. We should learn as the song says:

Nothing's impossible I have found,

For when my chin is on the ground,

I pick myself up,

Dust myself off,

And start all over again.

Rejection is even more difficult to accept than criticism. You have sweated away for months or even longer, you have drafted, re-drafted and re-drafted again, you have agonised over it and finally you have sent your precious manuscript to a publisher. You receive no acknowledgement and one day six months later or even longer, you come home one afternoon with not a care in the world and there on the floor in the hall under the letter-box is a large thick brown envelope. Your heart sinks, your hopes, perhaps buoyed from not having heard for so long, are shattered. You don't even want to open it to read the publisher's letter of rejection that will almost certainly wish you well with having it published elsewhere. A sensitive editor will occasionally say something encouraging, but this is rare. You don't care that the manuscript of the first book of James Joyce, JK Rowling or Maeve Binchy was rejected ten, fifteen or however many times. Though your heart is in your boots you have no option but to pick another suitable publisher and send it away again. As Maeve Binchy says: 'No publisher is going to break into your house, invade your study, rifle your desk, find the manuscript and say: "I've found it, just what I've been looking for."' You may wonder if you will live long enough before you die for ten or fifteen publishers to take six months or more each to reject your work, so perhaps you should leave instructions for your children to continue the process after you've gone!

Writing is sometimes no fun; it is hard slog and persistence, but when you succeed it is satisfying and fulfilling. There is no feeling like it and all the hard work will have been worth it. Your friends will see your published work and some will expect a free copy or even ask to borrow one! If your work is non-fiction some will expect to have been mentioned in it. Some may even buy a copy but none of them will have a bull's notion what has gone into the making of it.

CHAPTER 5. POETRY

Poetry is not to everyone's taste; in fact many people are indifferent or antipathetic to it. This may be the result of poor experience of poetry at school. If this is so for you, I urge you to try again. As I have already mentioned, I write some.

I wondered how I could start this chapter and keep it interesting for everybody. I thought I might start with an account of how I came to write poetry but then I thought of the foreword to a poetry collection of mine *The Rectory Dog*. I decided this might reassure readers of my good intentions more than a spiel about poetry in general. The spiel will follow but it should offer practical insight, in light of the foreword, to those who press on.

The foreword summarises succinctly my involvement with writing poetry:

"The first verse I ever wrote was when I was at boarding school aged thirteen. It was about homesickness and it was published in the school magazine. During my late teens and early twenties when I worked in Dublin and subsequently when I was at Trinity I wrote the occasional poem, but didn't show them to anybody. Over the years I continued to write sporadically until I had accumulated quite a few poems that I hadn't shown to anybody apart from Hilary, my wife.

In 1994 I decided to find out once and for all if what I wrote was in fact poetry at all or not. I sent a selection of what I had accumulated to Brendan Kennelly, one of Ireland's best known poets and Professor of Modern English Literature at Trinity College, Dublin, whom I knew from my time in Trinity. Recently I came across a quote of Edith Sitwell: 'A lot of people writing poetry today would be better employed keeping rabbits.' Had I known this quotation then I would have used it and asked him to tell me honestly if I would 'be better employed keeping rabbits.' What in fact I did ask him was similar. I asked him to tell me honestly if what I sent him was poetry, and that I wouldn't be in the least offended if he told me that I would be better off digging the garden.

To my great surprise Brendan wrote to me as follows:

"I want to tell you how much I enjoyed your poems – from the moment I read 'The Optimistic Thistledown' I was enjoying myself. It's the humour, the humanity, the truly delicious irony, the wit (especially of some of the shorter pieces) which has a genuine metaphysical touch – all this makes your poems very, very attractive. They're very serious too, but have that lovely light touch that Kavanagh always held is the mark of true poetry. He may be right. In any case I hope you continue to write; you should do readings (for some friends perhaps to begin with) – and I know that these poems, very many of them, would give pleasure to many people. I can only say I was genuinely delighted by them."

With such an encouraging reply I did as Brendan suggested; I continued to write. I didn't pursue his other suggestion that I 'should do readings, (perhaps for friends to begin with)'. His letter did, however, give me the confidence to read the odd poem when we had friends in, if it were pertinent to a topic we were discussing. I am particularly grateful to Brendan for his encouragement.

I am also grateful to Mike Byrne of Stonebridge Publications for publishing this collection, and for his professional help with the finer points of preparing poems for publication. I learned anew the meaning of the aphorism 'a poem is never finished, it's abandoned.'

[With the kind permission of Stonebridge Press]

It seems that every poet that ever lived has ventured their own definition of poetry. Here are some of them, and all say something of importance about what poetry is:

Alexander Pope:

'It can do most things that prose can do – tell stories, summon up physical prescriptions, develop arguments, stir the emotions, but it has another important task: to speak to the part of the imagination that is susceptible to the patterning of sounds.'

Boris Pasternak:

'Poetry searches for music amidst the tumult of the dictionary.'

Robert Frost:

'It is a momentary stay against confusion.'

Tolstoy talked about a mystery that can only be penetrated by poetry.

George Samson in his *Concise Cambridge History of English Literature* talking about Goldsmith's *Deserted Village* says:

'The way of poetry is to transfigure particulars and recreate them into abiding truths.'

Kenneth Koch, an American poet who died recently said that every word has a little music which poetry arranges so that it can be heard

Koch in his excellent book *Making Your Own Days, The Pleasures of Reading and Writing Poetry* also said that poetry is often regarded as a mystery. Nobody is quite sure where it comes from nor what it is, and nobody knows how anyone is able to write it.

Michael Longley famously concurs:

'If I knew where poetry came from I would go there.'

As you will have gathered, getting published is a chancy and hazardous business. I had previously sent the poetry collection that Stonebridge eventually published as *The Rectory Dog* to Dedalus Press and received a reply to say they had just ceased publishing and that I should try Gallery Press or Salmon Press. The response from Salmon was silence; I never heard a word, and I had a letter from Gallery saying that the writer didn't see in what I had submitted something they would want to publish, and wondering was he missing something.

I thought he could have let me down a little more gently.

I sent six poems to 'SHOp' a poetry magazine about which John Montague said 'The SHOp looks like being the best poetry magazine in these islands.' I had a note back from them to say: 'We're delighted with your poems, and would like to use ….' They chose and published three of them. Subsequently I sent them a dozen or more poems in batches of three or four at a time of what I considered my best poems over a period of a year and they declined them all. I cannot escape the conclusion that I have written only three poems of any real merit. I am fascinated, not a little amused and not in the slightest put out by evaluations of my poetry. It may be that there is only a grain or two of wheat amongst the chaff.

I do have a problem, however, about some modern poetry that is not, as it is said, very accessible. I know that poetry that is not immediately understood and demands some effort on the part of the reader may have greater rewards than poetry that is more readily accessible. None the less some modern poetry goes too far. It counts itself out for me by using obscure references, implications and inferences that the reader may not know. Now here is a piece of sacrilege or heresy: one such example is Derek Mahon's *A Disused Shed in County Wexford*. This poem is acknowledged by the cognoscenti to be a significant modern poem, a classic. I couldn't make much of it until I acquired a copy of Tom Paulin's *The Secret Life of Poems* in which he analyses and, as it were, demythologises the poem. After many readings with Paulin's help I could see what the poem was about and appreciate something of its worth. Ralph Waldo Emerson said: 'Unless you are a genius it's better to be comprehensible.' Maybe Derek Mahon is a genius.

I believe that much of the first rank of poetry written today is written by poets for poets and cognoscenti, and this excludes many thoughtful intelligent readers. Poets have only themselves to blame that only a tiny minority of people read poetry and some people are positively antagonistic to it. (I have one friend who told me he would be devastated if his son took to poetry.) None the less I am somewhat ambivalent about this since the work of an eminently accessible poet like for example John Betjeman does pall after a while and doesn't leave as powerful an impression as a poem that needs a lot of work to appreciate. I'm also aware that if the impressionists and post-impressionists had not painted as they did and had kept to art that was acceptable by the public, art would have stagnated and we would not have some of the world's most wonderful paintings. Though interesting in the history of the development of art, and no doubt of great significance to art insiders, if Picasso, the cubists, surrealists and expressionists had never existed, it wouldn't bother me in the slightest. As far as I'm concerned this also holds good for some modern poets too.

Several years ago the Arts Council of England looked into how the audience for poetry might be increased. They concluded that the value and purpose of poetry was in crisis. New readers were failing to breach the barriers created by the poetry world itself. They maintained that verse was badly presented, branded itself overly academic and took more notice of its creators than it did of its customers. Despite apparent popularity in some quarters, poetry had become a private art amongst consenting adults.

I don't, however, go as far as backwoodsmen who say it isn't poetry if it doesn't rhyme. If that were the case a good deal of the work of the great poets since the seventeenth century is not poetry. This position is promoted by no less a journal than the *Literary Review* which runs poetry competitions on given topics and stipulates that entries must rhyme, scan and make sense. This was the prejudice of the one-time editor Auberon Waugh. So boring do I find this rhyming, scanning poetry that makes sense, written on a set topic, that I consider it to be without any merit and I never read it.

I wrote the following poem to make my general point about some modern poetry:

THE POEM

When I read poetry,

I like to be able

to make some sense

of what I'm reading.

I write the odd poem myself

but I've no idea

where they come from,

and how it is

I am able to write them.

However, I have recently concluded

that my poetry will not develop

until it becomes,

at least partly, un-understandable.

Since I have an ambition,

before I die,

to write a really good

piece of poetry,

one day I suspended my reason

and wrote a poem

that came from the pit of my stomach;

the very depths of my being.

I had achieved my ambition.

A few days later

I took out the poem

to read it again,

and, believe it or not,

I hadn't the foggiest notion

what it was about.

No matter how often I read it

I couldn't make sense of it,

so I entered the poem for a competition

and won first prize.

At the prize-giving,

after the judges had spoken,

I thanked them and read the work.

Then I told the assembled company

that if any of them had the remotest idea

what it was about,

I would be most grateful

if they would kindly let me know.

In the circumstances,

I believe I'm entitled to say

that either the judges

were a bunch of blithering idiots,

> *or I am, in fact, a poetic genius.*
> *I am as sure as I can be*
> *that the latter is not the case,*
> *for if it were,*
> *I would not be wasting my time*
> *writing the foregoing nonsense.*

When Theo Dorgan had read the collection that included this poem he wrote to me:

> *'I like the wickedness of 'The Poem', tho' I hope it's as tongue in cheek as it seems to be.'*

I replied to say that it was, but in hindsight I'm not so sure. I did in fact write such an un-understandable poem.

> *The Dora bates the breath of storm*
> *upon the farthest hills,*
> *and back upon*
> *the cordless yarn*
> *returns another emptiness.*
> *The vacuous but enthralling sign*
> *of all that stood*
> *'tween gall of guilt*
> *and yesteryear*
> *constructs a tower*
> *of all that might have been*
> *if westward winds*
> *had left the headlands*
> *under cloudless skies.*

If any reader has even the foggiest notion what this poem is about, I'd be most grateful if they would let me know!

Coleridge in *Biographia Literaria* writes:

'I enjoyed the inestimable advantage of a very sensible, though at the same time, a very severe master.... In the truly great poets, he would say, there is a reason assignable, not only for every word, but for the position of every word.... he showed no mercy to phrase, metaphor, or image, unsupported by sound sense, or where the same sense might have been conveyed with equal force and dignity in plainer words.'

Danish scientist, mathematician and poet, Piet Hein, in one of his short pithy poems wrote:

> *A poet should be of the*
> *old-fashioned meaningless brand:*
> *obscure, esoteric, symbolic,-*
> *the critics demand it;*
> *so if there is a poem of mine*
> *that you do understand*
> *I'll gladly explain what it means*
> *till you don't understand it.*

American poet J.V. Cunningham talking about why he particularly liked a piece he had written said it was because it was all denotation and no connotation; because it had only one level of meaning; because it was not ironic, paradoxical, complex, or subtle; and because the meter [sic] was monotonously regular.'

Over the years I kept hearing that in Dublin there were what were described as 'gangs' of poets all looking down on each other. I had an insight into something of this when in a letter to me a well-known poet made a derogatory passing allusion to another well-known poet. I asked Theo Dorgan about the gangs and he replied:

Trust me, Dublin is not awash with poetry gangs or factions; I've been listening to that kind of talk for decades, and I can assure you that whoever might mug you on your travels it won't be a gang of poets. There are plenty of people in the world around poetry who feel superior to everyone else, but I hadn't noticed them forming up in gangs! In my time I've met TDs, PDs, tax inspectors, Hannibal Lectors, bus drivers and career skivers who consider themselves superior to everybody else, and I never pay them a blind bit of notice.'

I'm sure that the world of poetry is no different from the world of any of the arts, so a neophyte in any of them needs to keep an ear to the ground.

I met Mike Byrne of Stonebridge Publications through friends in County Clare. He was from Clare but living and publishing in Wales. I sent him a bundle of poems. He decided that he would publish a collection and selected 64 of them for *The Rectory Dog*. If you are not just skimming through this book you will have read the foreword above quoting Brendan Kennelly. Mike is an affable, laid back individual who rolls his own cigarettes. He makes his books by hand and tells us in a leaflet inserted into all of them:

A handmade book,…. has been touched by hand many times over during its construction. The paper is fed into the printing press by hand; the printed sheets are held in the hand and examined for errors and flaws: the sheets are collated, punched, stitched, glued and trimmed – all by hand,… The boards for the cover, the end-papers, the binding cloth and the final covering are all individually cut by hand and assembled to make the 'case' to receive the finished pages…. Unlike its machine made counterpart the hand-made book has individuality. It has character.

Mike takes great pride in his work and tells us that every one of his books is an individual. Like most craftsmen he cannot be rushed even when he is weeks behind schedule. The writer must be patient. I saw proofs and covers but didn't see a book until a few minutes before the launch was due to start. Mike brought the books to Ireland himself, but on the way he went to see family in Clare. On the evening of the launch he travelled from Limerick by train. People were starting to arrive; the room was filling up and no sign of Mike or books. It was lashing rain. A few minutes before the scheduled start Mike arrived, drenched. He deposited the books in the room to be unwrapped ready for sale and went outside for a smoke. In his own time he arrived into the crowded room and spoke eloquently about the collection, as is the habit of publishers at the launch of their own books. The guest speaker, Leo Cullen, a writer and friend of mine, whom I had invited to speak, warmly commended it as naturally I expected he would. As you can imagine it would be highly unusual or probably unknown for a guest invited to launch a book to speak other than exuberantly about it.

Chapter 6. Dealing with Publishers

My first memoir *Believe It Or Not* had been successful. There was a second printing; it was the second-best seller of the publisher in the first six months of its publication. I had written it to give a picture of what it was like to have been brought up and lived in the tiny less than five per cent minority Protestant community in the South of Ireland from the 1940s onward. A sub-theme was my growing doubts about belief. When I had finished writing *That Could Never Be*, the book that I had ghost written, I decided to write another memoir of my own from the opposite perspective to the first. It would show how the tiny Protestant community viewed and was affected by the large, ninety-five per cent plus, Catholic community. It would also discuss how I found that I no longer believed the essential doctrines of the Christian Faith.

When I had finished it I submitted it to a publisher. It contained all new material. In a few weeks I had a phone call from him. He said he had read the manuscript and that it was anti-Catholic. He asked me to call to discuss it. I made an appointment. When I arrived for the meeting some five or six weeks after our telephone conversation, the publisher had one of his senior staff with him.

After the formalities he put the manuscript down on the desk in front of me and said:

'We feel the format doesn't work.'

I was surprised since the reason he gave on the phone was that it was anti-Catholic. I asked him what I could do to improve it. He shrugged his shoulders and said: 'I don't know.' It was clear that he wasn't interested in talking about it. I said:

'I thought you said it was anti-Catholic?' He picked up the manuscript and while he was flicking through it I turned to his colleague and asked him his opinion of some particular point in the text. He was somewhat nonplussed and obviously didn't know the point to which I had referred and said:

'I only speed read part of it.' I then turned back to the publisher who read the following passage, I assumed as an example of my anti-Catholicism, now that I had reminded him of what he had said:

'It seems that Roman Catholicism seeks to keep a tight control on its members and has an extensive catechism and canon law for achieving this, while for instance Anglicanism has a simple catechism and a minimum of canon law.'

To me this was simply factual and could hardly be construed as anti-Catholic. I soon realised that, regardless, the publisher had made a non-negotiable decision not to publish. His complete lack of interest was confirmed to me by his standing there admiring his finger nails. I had the distinct impression that he wished I would go. I thanked him and his colleague and left. I sat in the car in the carpark to make some notes and to try to make sense of the meeting when it dawned on me. I had been naive.

The memoir was critical of some aspects of Catholicism but in a balanced way. How could anybody write an account of the Catholic Church's attitude to Protestants in Ireland in its triumphalist period up to the Second Vatican Council without being critical? However, my criticism was reasoned and balanced. Such criticism might not be pleasing to devout Catholics who bought the devotional material this publisher published and the memoir would in general be in conflict with his list. I had also been critical in places of the Church of Ireland and the publisher might have felt that this and the declaration in the book of my no longer believing would not help sales. With these points in mind I began to realise that in his position I might not have published the book either, not because it was anti-Catholic or because the format wouldn't work, but because it might not have been a wise business decision.

Some short time later I was on the phone to the publisher's colleague who by his own admission had 'only speed read part of it.' I said something about the meeting and that perhaps rejection had to do with the fact that the company published a lot of devotional Catholic material and that the publisher's comment about the manuscript being 'anti-Catholic' had something to do with that. He denied this and referred to the manuscript as a mishmash. How he knew this when, by his own admission, he hadn't read it (apart from speed reading part of it) I didn't know. Perhaps it was something the publisher had said to him. The truth is that it was not a mishmash. It had a perfectly ordered memoir time sequence. I asked a friend, an English Literature graduate and a competent critic, if she thought it was a mishmash. She read it and told me that it was a better book than the first memoir.

Before sending the manuscript to another publisher I sent it to a friend, Michael Burrows, whom I knew would be ruthlessly honest with me, and asked him to say if he thought I had been anti-Catholic. Amongst other things in a positive and comprehensive overall critique he said:

'You offer a very fair yet honest description of how members of the C of I and the majority Church perceived each other and the beliefs each Church held dear in those bye-gone days. No one could say you are anti-Catholic – indeed you have a laudable capacity to be amused by the antics of the Church of Ireland, but you do show how in the midst of an apparent peaceful neighbourliness there really were two worlds and each world somehow feared the assumptions and the mindset of the other.'

I then sent the manuscript, unaltered, along with a copy of the first memoir for information to two publishers I will call 'Speedy' and 'Even Faster'. I had a very civil letter of acknowledgement from 'Speedy' saying it might be as long as six months before they would be in touch. Not having heard from them two years and four months later, I phoned to know what the position was. They looked it up and told me that they had rejected that manuscript over a year before; eighteen months after I had submitted it. I asked politely why they didn't let me know.

'That was a mistake,' and the publisher apologised. I received a letter of apology in the post two days later. If you think that was bad, read on.

The second of these two publishers was 'Even Faster.' His stated time for decision on a manuscript was three months; a short period in the publishing world. About six months after I had submitted the manuscript to him I phoned to know when I would have news one way or the other. He promised me that he would be in touch in the New Year, about three months away. In the following June, a year after I had submitted it in the first place, I phoned again. He promised that he would be in touch before Christmas. No word. I phoned again some months later. He would have word at the end of the summer. The summer came and went. I decided not to phone and called unannounced to his office. He was apologetic and gave me another of his many excuses.

Sometime after this 'Even Faster' phoned me and said he had lost the copy of my first memoir that I had given him, and could I send him another. I did. Some months later I received, without any comment from him, by e-mail a copy of a reader's report he had commissioned. It was a very good report fulsomely commending the manuscript. I was delighted. Months later I had heard nothing so I phoned again and said I would like to know the situation.

'I'm still interested,' he said, 'but if you want to submit to another publisher, do.' Encouraged by the reader's report I decided to wait, but eventually sent a copy of the manuscript to another publishing house. One year later I had heard nothing from this publisher either, so I phoned to be told that they had no record of having received a manuscript from me but they would make a search. Two days later an editor phoned and said that independently of my enquiry, by coincidence, she was clearing out the office of a staff member who had left the company some months before and had found the manuscript. She would read it immediately and let me know in two weeks. She was as good as her word. She phoned and asked to meet me when she told me they would publish the anti-Catholic mishmash with the format that wouldn't work. There was still no word from the other mutt. He had broken his word to me four times in three years. When I pointed this out to him subsequently he at least had the decency to say:

'I know. I'm ashamed of myself.'

I didn't contact him when the second company said they would publish and just before publication of the memoir entitled *The Rector Who Wouldn't Pray For Rain* I had an e-mail from him to say that he was no longer interested. He had kept me dangling for over three years.

'Why,' you may ask, 'did you not use a literary agent? Publishers would not treat an agent like this. Furthermore an agent would know the publishers most likely to be interested in a particular manuscript.' My answer: 'Yes, I'd love to be able to talk about "my agent," but it's not as easy as it sounds. I tried.'

One literary agent declined to take the first manuscript, the one that was published in which I agreed to the archiepiscopal and two other deletions. Some time later I asked him if he would read the manuscript of a novel. When I described it to him he told me that he was inundated at the moment and it would take a long time before he would get to it, but he would read it in a matter of weeks for a fee. Reflecting that sooner or later I would have to die, and that this unhappy occurrence might take place before the reading public would have access to my masterpiece, I opted for the fee. In due course the agent phoned and I went to see him. He declined to take on the manuscript, but I had forgotten the paper and pencil he had asked me to bring. He gave me some paper and treated me like a schoolboy as he proceeded to read out for me to take down copy editing emendations that he had made.

I submitted a manuscript sometime later to another literary agent and when I phoned about six months later they had lost it so I sent them another copy. I contacted them in another six months (with agents and publishers I tend to deal in periods of six months) to be told over the phone that they were not taking on any new authors.

I suspect that agents don't want to handle small circulation manuscripts no matter how good they are. They want manuscripts with large sales potential that will generate significant commission. This is understandable; they have to make a living. Given the choice, I suspect that most of them would prefer to handle 'chick lit,' or 'popular romance' as its authors call it, no matter how lightweight, with vast sales potential, to novels of literary merit with small sales. A manuscript of mine would not fall into either category.

I sometimes go around the place muttering to myself over and over again: 'Publishers are shysters, publishers are shysters ...' This probably isn't fair despite the fact that they all claim to have to deal with fifty-seven million or more unsolicited manuscripts a year. Publishers are the same as any group of people who do the same job. They are not a distinct species. They are human beings so there are all sorts. I have received formal letters of rejection, pleasant letters of rejection, some helpful and kindly letters of rejection and one downright offensive one. The traditional publisher's rejection slip seems to be a thing of the past. I've heard it talked about, but I've never been rejected by one.

It would be good to have the attitude of Mrs Turkin in Chekhov's short story *Ionych*:

'Do you publish your works in periodicals?' Startsev asked Mrs Turkin.
'No' she replied, 'I don't publish them anywhere. I write them and put them away in a cupboard. Why publish them?' she exclaimed. 'We're well enough off.'

Despite Dr Johnson and Mrs Turkin, being published for most of us is not primarily about money, it's about ego.

Having had one poetry collection published, I decided to try another as I still had a stack of unpublished poems. I sent them all off to Mike Byrne of Stonebridge. He selected fifty-six of them to publish as a second collection. As it happened I would be on a cargo ship on the way to the West Indies when the proofs were due to be ready for correction. It was theoretically possible for me to receive them in the middle of the Atlantic, but it would be impractical. I asked Suzanne, my novelist friend, an experienced teacher of creative writing, to liaise with Mike and correct the proofs for me. She readily agreed and I gave her total power of literary attorney. I told her that Mike was a relaxed guy; the kind whose 'tomorrow' was usually located somewhere in the third or fourth week hence. When I arrived home all the work had been done, proofs had been corrected and amongst some minor corrections Suzanne and Mike had conspired together to leave out the last verse of one of the poems. The cheek of them; I was taken aback, but in no time I realised that they had been absolutely right. There is a place for critics and editors, as writers can easily lose the run of themselves!

The collection, *A Narrow Escape* was published; another fine hand-bound production. Mike wasn't able to attend the launch, but he had done his bit in writing the blurb:

His popular first collection of poetry, The Rectory Dog, was a distinct success with readers and critics alike, and became Stonebridge's best selling poetry volume for the year of its first publication, 2006. Now comes A Narrow Escape, full of sharp humour, deep insight and witty pithy comments on the state of the world and everyone in it.

When I read the blurb all of this was news to me! You need to know about publishers' blurbs. Facts they write are probably true, but for opinion many of them are prepared to write anything that will encourage the browser to buy the book. If possible a publisher will ask a well-known literary figure or two to say what they can for the blurb without sinning their souls, in order to commend the book and encourage people to buy it. Did you ever see a piece of negative criticism in a blurb from a famous name? If Mike had sent a copy to Seamus Heaney for a comment for the blurb, which I needn't tell you he didn't, and Heaney had written 'this is a collection of trivial verse half of which is no more than mangled prose,' Nobel Prize or no Nobel Prize do you think Mike would have used it? Of course he wouldn't. It's the job of publishers to make the best fist they can to make money in order to stay in business and make a livelihood. No matter what hyperbole their blurbs contain it is in the interest of writers to support publishers or we would all be likely to end up like Mrs Turkin, putting our manuscripts away in cupboards but for a different reason; there would be fewer publishers around to publish them.

Frank Kelly who played Father Jack, the drunken lecherous old priest in *Father Ted* was to have launched the collection, but at the last minute he was not able. Suzanne who had worked with Mike proof-reading the collection kindly agreed to do the honours. Since there is such an infinitesimal market for poetry, especially by unknowns, and Stonebridge does not sell through bookshops, each author is retailer for his or her own work.

Chapter 7. More Publishers

After the memoirs I started a novel. I knew no more about the structure or theory of the novel then than I knew about the structure of the short story when I sat down and wrote *Bill's Wife*. Most people don't know the theory of riding bicycles when they start to ride one; balance, velocity and to pull up the back brake rather than the front one so that they won't go over the handlebars and end up in a heap on the ground. Over the years I had read a fair share of novels and had an instinct for how they worked. You can drive a car for years and not have the foggiest notion about the theory of the internal combustion engine, but when it doesn't work you have to find somebody who does.

I had always heard that first novels, although fiction, are usually autobiographical in character. My first, and possibly only, novel was autobiographical in character. I give below a brief summary of what it is about.

I wanted to show what life can really be like for Church of Ireland rectors and to expose the human beings behind the job. I also wanted to give a voice to those people whose life is religion and who find they are forced to reassess their own beliefs. There are expectations laid upon the rectory family that puts them in a different category from 'ordinary people'. When the child of a rector gets into trouble at school, a teacher will often say: '….and your father a clergyman'. People who live in rectories are as human as anybody else. 'There is no greater heresy than that the office sanctifies the holder of it.' This is as true for the rector's wife as it is for the rector. The novel is made up of transient beings. Some come from the past and pass through the present and some in the present refuse to leave the past. The rector's life is changing in ways he does not yet understand. How long does this idyllic rectory in the heart of rural Ireland in the 1970's hide the secrets of those who live behind its walls?

When I had finished I asked my novelist friend to read it for me. She made suggestions one of which was that I needed a sub-plot, so I added one. When I had done the best I was able with it I sent it to two publishers.

The first one complimented the standard of writing, the depth of learning and earnestness of purpose which he said was not evident in many scripts that land on his desk. He complimented the selfless immersion of the author in the lives of the characters in the best John McGahern and Brian Moore tradition. He averred that the novel was a little too 'quiet', and feared it might not find its target audience. He wished me well in placing it elsewhere.

The second publisher said that their readers had many positive comments to make about the novel: the interesting characters and locations, the high standard of writing and the original plot. They felt that the various elements didn't quite come together as a whole and wished me all the best in securing publication elsewhere.

It is great to receive all the compliments but then your heart sinks when you arrive at the 'unfortunately' or the 'however.' Subsequently I sent the first three chapters and a synopsis to another publisher.

This one said that they didn't think the novel was ready for publication. They said that it was well written and the synopsis indicated a strong story, but that it needed some editing and re-working. They thought there was too much 'telling' and not enough 'showing'. They suggested that I might try making it a third person narrative.

In the last paragraph of their letter they said that I was free, of course, to ignore all their comments that other publishers might think differently. They affirmed that it was a potentially good novel, but needed more work, and wished me well with it.

These three letters were, in my experience, most unusual. Letters of rejection usually say that the publisher is not accepting the manuscript for publication and wishes you well in placing it elsewhere. Simple as that; a few sentences. As you have seen earlier the occasional publisher will tell you a cock-and-bull story and others will keep you waiting for over three years before they reject your manuscript. These three publishers took the trouble to say something helpful to the author which is very unusual. The third one is exceptional, if not unique, in that the editor took a great deal of trouble to write a very full and helpful critique. You could use it as a model for critiquing your own work. I wrote and thanked this writer for the trouble she had taken. How embarrassing that she had to point out the 'show don't tell' principle to me which I spend my time these days pointing out to students I teach! I believe that much of my 'tell' was necessary. With some of her critique I was in agreement and took it on board. With some I wasn't and held a different opinion; I thought, for example, that if written in the third person it would lose more than it would gain.

While on the subject of publishers, there is another point to make about some of them. In my experience they are not good at keeping in touch with their authors. One year my royalties cheque was three months overdue. I phoned to enquire. The cheque arrived in a couple of days accompanied by a letter of abject apology for the oversight from the managing director, and saying it would not happen again. The cheque included an item 'Polish Deposit.' I had no idea to what it was that this referred. I phoned to ask. A Polish publisher had paid a deposit to have the right to translate the work into Polish and my publisher didn't bother to tell me. I looked forward to seeing a Polish copy of the book. It never happened. The recession hit and the Polish publisher forfeited his deposit.

Two years later my royalties cheque from the same publisher was one month late. I phoned and the cheque arrived in the post again with an apology for being late. I have no doubt that these days some publishers are just hanging in there financially and it is in the interest of writers to support them to see that they do.

Some authors re-write novels half a dozen or more times. I had sent this one to about ten publishers. I hadn't the stomach or the energy to re-write it again and I left it there. I wasn't sure that I would ever get back to it. I'm sorry to say I thought it might well go down with the ship. To paraphrase the bard when he says: 'Full many a flower is born to blush unseen and waste its sweetness on the desert air.' Full many a manuscript is written to lie unpublished and waste its brilliance in a bottom drawer, with respect to Maeve Binchy. There is no excuse for not persisting. I tell you all of this in order to encourage you **not** to follow my example. Stick with it, re-write, re-write again – a dozen times if that's what it takes. Put in the hard work and don't forget – if you don't do it, nobody else will.

In recent years I had heard much talk about self-publishing and had dismissed it as an option for me on the principle that I had always said I would never publish anything I had written other than in the conventional way with a commercial publisher. I came across the name of an English publisher from a novel that Hilary was reading. I sent them a summary of *Jennifer* which I had re-named *The Rectory*, and asked if I might send them the manuscript. They wrote back as follows:

Thank you for your enquiry.

It is important to understand from the start that we are a "print on demand" publishing company. We publish the book, get it recorded in the British Library and get it listed with Amazon and other online retailers for sale. We do not do traditional print runs and distribution of books to shops. If a book is sold it is printed on demand and delivered to the customer whether this is a shop or an individual, thus negating the need for stock or large print runs. While the main target is online sales, bookshops can still order the book through their wholesalers.

We do not offer any critical analysis of the work or interfere with the content.

We do not market the book for you. It is up to the author to market and promote the book.

We are happy to talk to you and give you advice – we are just as happy as you when you sell books.

The author is expected to do the final proof read and approve the product ready for printing.

The author pays the set up costs of the book - the basic set up is £500 + VAT.

This includes:

- typesetting the book,
- a PDF version of your book emailed to you prior to printing
- 5 copies of your book
- An ISBN (International Standard Book Number)
- Listed on Amazon and other online retailers
- Wholesale distribution through Gardners, Bertrams and Ingram
- Placed on legal deposit with the British Library

We will design a cover if you do not already have one – if you require specific work done on the cover this will have to be discussed and priced.

You are not obliged to buy any books although the facility exists for you to order copies of your book and we would encourage you to order some for practical review, marketing and personal sales purposes.

The advantage of this no frills model is that the author takes away a higher percentage of the sales and exercises full artistic control over the work.

I see you have published books before and you are probably realistic about sales. Writing a great book does not guarantee financial success these days. We do not offer advance payments of any kind. You get a slice of every book sold – normally consolidated into 6 month financial periods in arrears.

If this sort of arrangement is what you are looking for please send us your manuscript in both hard and soft copy and we will have a look at it.

My instinct from this letter was that this was an honest publisher offering a very reasonable deal. They were being entirely upfront and I had a copy of their work from which I could see that their finished product was first class. It was clear that they were not one of those so-called 'vanity publishers' who promise you that your work could very well be reviewed in the national press, that it could sell many thousands of copies, the ones who praise an author's manuscript to the skies before asking for an exorbitant fee to assist with the printing and ask you to sign a contract that involves the author in buying a large number of copies which he or she could not possibly sell.

A fella' is entitled to change his mind and I'm very glad that I did. They published successfully *The Rectory*, now re-named *Transient Beings*, and a manuscript on cargo ship voyaging, called *Curious Cargo* that I describe below. They produced two first class cover designs and chose two excellent titles. During the process they made a number of good suggestions, and all along the line they consulted with me and explained clearly the reasons for the suggestions they made. I could not speak highly enough of them.

There is also e-publishing the details of which I know nothing. Students keep telling me about it. I believe that it is well worth exploring and I encourage you do so. One of the bonuses of e-publishing is that it gives access to world-wide markets, as does the method of the publishers of *Transient Beings* and *Curious Cargo*.

It is not widely known that some cargo ships carry a small number of passengers. Hilary and I have recently been on two cargo ship voyages. One was for five weeks to the Caribbean, South and Central America and the second was a four week voyage into the Mediterranean. My next project was to write an account of our experiences on these ships.

In addition to creating the atmosphere experienced by passengers on a freighter I gave accounts of our time ashore and the background to the places we visited. All but a couple of our ports of call gave us access to places of interest. On the first voyage crossing the Atlantic we were nine days out of sight of land, and this too is an experience when interest centres on the human dynamic within the ship, apart from keeping an eye out for whales and other ships.

Long periods at sea give one plenty of time to think and I included my own reflections on politicians, bankers, developers, the media and such matters. To gaze at the stars on a cloudless night from the deck of a freighter in the middle of the Atlantic inevitably gives rise to questions about the world, the universe, meaning, purpose and life itself and I commented on these weighty matters too.

Our ports of call on the first voyage were Dover, Antwerp, Le Havre, Guadeloupe, Martinique, (both West Indies), Turbo (Colombia), Panama, Moin (Costa Rica) and The Azores. This voyage was not all plain sailing but this added greatly to the experience. The second voyage was Southampton, Salerno (Italy), Piraeas (Greece), Izmir (Turkey), Limassol (Cyprus), Alexandria (Egypt), Ashdod (Israel), Salerno again, Savona (Italy), Setubal (Portugal) and Bristol.

This is not just a travel book but a work reflecting on many things while travelling by cargo vessel and all that that entails. It was rejected by four publishers. When I come into the house having been out all day, I dread finding on the floor under the letter-box that large brown envelope containing the returned manuscript and a polite letter of rejection, knowing that there's nothing for it but to send it out again until I run out of publishers. I never get used to rejection, but I do wonder from time to time how such intelligent people as most publishers are can so easily pass up such wonderful pieces of world class literature!

As a result of my first memoir having been launched in Wexford I established a relationship with the County Library in the town. They asked me to do an evening of readings from the memoir and in due course to do some poetry readings. Later on the library asked me to conduct a day-long poetry seminar during a literature week. It took place at the old St Peter's College in the town and at the same time along the passage Suzanne Power was conducting a seminar on the novel. This was the first time I had met her. At the lunch interval in the restaurant we had a most congenial conversation. In addition to being a warm person she is a successful novelist, journalist and teacher of creative writing. She has a warm open personality and she is a great enthusiast and encourager. Subsequently I asked her to launch my second memoir, *The Rector Who Wouldn't Pray For Rain*, also in Wexford.

She shared the teaching of a creative writing course at the Kilkenny campus of the National University of Ireland Maynooth with John MacKenna, novelist and short story writer. One taught the short story and creative non-fiction and the other the novel. So successful was the course that Maynooth wanted to have the same course on the home campus but John didn't have time to teach it.

One night I was sitting at home, minding my own business, when the phone rang. It was Suzanne. She was in Dublin and asked if she could call around. I was delighted to see her, and then the question: would I teach the short story and creative non-fiction part of the Maynooth course? It would be an evening course in the Adult Education Department. Nothing could have been further from my consideration of what I could do. To write the stuff myself was one thing, but I was aware that there was a lot of theory that I didn't know. It would be hard to teach instinct. She went away empty-handed. Some few weeks later she came back to see if she could encourage me to teach the course. In the meantime Hilary had tried to convince me that I could do it. The two ganged up so what chance had I? Finally I capitulated.

I had the whole summer to give to preparation and did an immense amount of work. None the less I was nervous about the prospect. I had a background in adult education and knew that if you weren't a bit nervous about teaching a particular course you wouldn't really do it well. In September a letter arrived from Maynooth to say that too few students had enrolled to justify putting on the course. I had mixed feelings. At one level I was mightily relieved and at another I was sorry that, having done the work in preparation, I would not be able to use it. On balance I was relieved. The preparation I had done was not wasted. I had learned a great deal that was useful for my own writing.

The following year fourteen people registered and the course went ahead. On the first night I was nervous but I knew I would not be as nervous as most of the students; adults experience anxiety coming new to formal learning situations. There were two men and twelve women and all had some facility to write. In no time the group had gelled and we had a great year together. The following year nineteen people registered – six men and thirteen women. This was the group I mentioned in the introduction. This was a particularly lively and spirited bunch of people and again we had a great year together. In the third year twenty-four students registered which was too many for workshop purposes, so I had two groups of twelve. This year there are seventeen in the class.

In Part II I will pass on what I have learned of creative writing from my own writing, my preparation for the Maynooth course and from four years of tutoring it.

The Craft

Chapter 1. Creative Writing

There are all kinds of people who write. You hear of children who at the age of five or six start to write stories. Some of these children stop writing at a later stage and some write throughout their lives. Other people start writing late in life; Mary Wesley wrote her first novel when she was seventy and she wrote ten novels during the next fourteen years. If you have the inclination to write it is never too late to start. On the other hand Robert Louis Stephenson and Anton Chekhov both died aged forty-four and Oscar Wilde died at forty-six.

Your Authentic Voice

The first thing you must do is to become aware of your own authentic voice. That is what it is you want to say to the world from your own unique life experience. In the majesty of this mysterious creation, however it came to be, what do you want to hold up for people to look at? Whatever that is must come from the person you really are, good bits and bad bits. It will come from your unconscious and your conscious. Using your authentic voice reveals who you truly are as a result of your life to date and this may take courage. In this world with so much beauty and potential for good but in which there is a preponderance of evil, pain and suffering that people inflict upon themselves or upon each other, what do you want to say from your unique experience? You can illustrate some of these profound matters in the simplest story. You may want to tell a story to say that despite everything it is love, romantic or otherwise, that makes life worthwhile, that doing things for other people is the only way of being authentically human. You may want to say that every person is out for themselves, and money and power are the ultimate human objectives. It is inevitable that you say something from the perspective of your own life, something that your life has given you as an insight that has meaning for you and that you want to tell to others. This is your voice. You don't necessarily say these things explicitly, but they become evident by how you tell the story.

Using Your Own Authentic Voice

Above all you must be honest and not be afraid of what people may think of you. You must risk. Very little of value is achieved without some risk. What you say must be what you really think, must come from deeper inside you than the superficial chat at which we spend much of our time.

You must have some care for your reader. You may want to say something radical that you know will not be popular with some, but you must not get at people, simply state your case.

We all have our own phrasings, expressions and patterns of speech. Use them. As you write don't try to imitate or be different from who you are. You will know that you have succeeded in this when somebody says to you: 'I read your piece and you might as well have been talking to me.' Use your own illustrations, similes and metaphors. Don't use the well-worn, clichéd ones that everybody uses.

The possibilities are infinite, but don't forget that although much has been said by writers over the centuries, nobody else who has ever lived or written has had your life experience. Nobody else can speak from your unique perspective. You must decide the story, fiction or non-fiction, which you tell to make your point. In either case what you say must be true to life, you must hold up something that is real in human experience. Even the most scientific of science fiction and the most fantastic of fantasy literature take place in the context of human motivations and human responses. It is unlikely that you will invent a new plot no matter how futuristic, fantastic or ordinary and everyday. It is believed that in all of literature there are seven basic plots and every story written is a variation of one kind or another on one of these. See Christopher Booker's *The Seven Basic Plots*. Furthermore your story must be about what is, and not what should or ought to be. You must not preach or moralise.

The tool you use is language; it is, as we said earlier, the stock in trade of the writer. Writing is not just inspiration and letting it flow. It is as much perspiration and hard work. Writing is a craft and that is what you need to learn. As in any branch of the arts this can be boring, plodding, tedious, technical and hard work. The musician of whatever instrument has to learn the techniques of his instrument and has to practise, and for professionals, hours every day. The concert pianist practises scales, arpeggios and études for as much as four or five hours every day. I'm sure they don't enjoy it, but it is necessary if they are to play well. The painter must learn the techniques of his art; use and application of paint, use of brushes, paper and canvas. He or she must practise different techniques in order to create paintings that are works of art.

So it is with creative writing, which is also an art. It is not simply a matter of inspiration and getting it down however it comes. There is the hard work of learning the craft of writing so that you have a sound familiarity with principles in order to be able to express your inspiration well.

There is a problem with writing that does not apply to the other arts: we use English every day. We write and speak English in all kinds of different situations. We are familiar with it but because we are familiar in this way and because we use it all the time we must not make the mistake of believing that it easy to write well. We don't necessarily write as we speak. We must learn the underlying craft of creative writing. If you don't want to do this boring, technical, theoretical and plodding work you won't write well and if you don't write well you won't be published which, unless you are a Mrs Turkin, is the prime objective.

In passing, when you do write in the course of your day, take care to write well, whether it is a shopping list, a note to leave on the kitchen table, an e-mail or whatever. Use capitals, punctuate, make paragraphs and cultivate the habit of writing properly. When you write an e-mail read it over more than once, before you send it. It is as easy to form good habits as bad ones. Try using English when writing texts rather than text language. Some chance!

Jennifer Johnston has said that the passages she writes that flow easily are the passages she alters, edits and often deletes altogether in subsequent drafts. The passages she agonises over and struggles to get down in the first place are the ones that endure and survive into the final work. Edna O'Brien has said that she often struggles for a whole afternoon to find the right word or phrase before she is happy with a sentence or passage. Dr Johnson said:

'what is written without effort is in general read without pleasure.'

Oscar Wilde said (amongst other things!):

There is no such thing as an immoral book; books are either well written or badly written.'

When your ideas are flowing get a draft down on paper; don't worry about punctuation, paragraphs and all the other things. Just get the ideas down. Then re-draft, add, delete and achieve a structure. Draft again if you are not satisfied. When you have the structure right then read and re-read 3, 4, 5 times to pick up all the things we will talk about as the principles of good writing. Then you need to leave it for a day or more; come back fresh to it, read it again and again and even then you will miss things but you will have reduced your mistakes to a minimum.

There are broadly three categories of English: vernacular English, Standard English and literary English. Vernacular English is everyday language used in the family, at work, at recreation or wherever. It includes unorthodox grammar and syntax, idiom, slang and swearing, the last of which is sometimes referred to as 'the vernacular.' This is not the language of narrative or exposition in creative writing. It is, of course, used in dialogue when it is the authentic language of the character portrayed and it is often used purposely to show something of character.

Some young people tend to use sloppy vernacular, for example a nineteen or twenty year old bank clerk to a customer making a lodgement: 'howya,' 'there ya go,' 'seeya.' What's wrong with 'good morning' or just 'morning,' 'here you are,' 'goodbye'? None of these are posh words, big words or unusual words. Fashions arise and become embedded in the use of language, for example the overuse of the word 'absolutely'. Inappropriate excess devalues language: handing you change when you have bought a newspaper the assistant says 'thanks a million' or 'brilliant'. None of this kind of language should appear in your writing except when appropriate in dialogue.

Standard English is the language of public discourse, journalism, broadcasting, business, scientific and academic writing and of most everyday use. It observes all the rules of grammar and syntax. The objective is clarity of communication. However the public discourse of politicians is often far from Standard English. Bertie Ahern, the former Taoiseach, while sounding plausible, sometimes spoke a brand of mangled English, whether by chance or by design it was hard to tell, but probably a bit of both, that made it difficult if not impossible to know what he was saying. It could flummox the listener and make it difficult for an interviewer to formulate the next question. On a panel programme on national television the issue arose as to whether Mr Ahern was the right man for a job in Europe. One of the participants asked if Mr Ahern spoke French. A voice from the far end of the panel was heard to say: 'No, he doesn't even speak English.'

On the other hand Guards for some reason speak an over formalised English.

For example, did you ever notice that Guards never 'go' anywhere; they 'proceed.' 'I proceeded up the road.' If 'go' was good enough for Yeats, Nobel Prize winner in Literature, and one of the finest poets in the English language; 'I will arise and go now and go to Inishfree,' twice in four words, I'm not sure why 'go' is not acceptable to the average Guard. 'I will arise and proceed now!'

Guards never start or begin anything; they 'commence'. 'We 'commenced' a search rather than we 'began' or 'started' a search. They never ask for 'help'. They ask for 'assistance'. Guards never find 'a man's body' or 'the body of a man'; they find the 'body of an adult male'.

When writing, use the common and shorter word rather than the unusual or longer word. Standard English is somewhere between the mangled English of Bertie Ahern and Garda-speak.

The purpose of literary English is not simply to communicate clearly, but of course it must do that. Barbara Loundsberry talks about 'a clear style with rhythm, texture, colour and dramatic pace.' Literary English uses metaphor, simile, and any literary device that contributes to a style that adds to the pleasure of reading. It is sometimes expansive in order to paint word pictures of people, places and events that are more than the mere statements of facts.

The following is an example of Standard English simply conveying facts:

We took our planned route and stayed near Brecon on Thursday night. We found a good restaurant that evening run by a New Zealander, whose grandfather came from Co Tipperary. He told us that when he was in his late teens he returned to the village of his grandfather's birth and received a wonderful welcome from his Irish cousins.

Now in literary English conveying more than the bare facts and written to create an atmosphere to add interest to the pleasure of the reader:

We made our way easily from Forest Lane to our planned route through Wales. On Thursday night we stayed in a guest house and found an excellent restaurant 'Tipple and Tiffin', tucked away at the back of the theatre in Brecon. It was owned and run by a Kiwi whose grandparents came from Borisokane, Co Tipperary.

He recounted to us his first visit there when he was eighteen and how he found some cousins. He had no idea how word had spread, but the house quickly filled with relations and friends who came to welcome the grandson of Paddy Bourke. At about midnight the whole company went down the darkened village to a shop that appeared to the naive youngster from the New World to be shut. A coded tap on the window led to the door being opened and the whole party went through to a passage that led to a crowded smoke-filled bar where he was again fêted as Paddy Bourke's grandson and in no time there were before him on the table more pints of stout than he would drink in a month.

Language changes and evolves. To see this all you have to do is read Shakespeare, Jane Austen or any author of a previous time. They use words and modes of expression that are no longer in use today, and yet we can derive great pleasure from reading them. Some Jane Austen dialogue is so stilted that it is hard to imagine that people at that time ever spoke so formally to each other, but they did.

If you have bought this book or if you sign on for a creative writing course, it is almost certain that you have some facility to write. It is extremely unlikely that you will do either of these things if you haven't something of the instinct to create in words. Like any natural facility, in trades, professions, in the arts, in sport or in any area of life this is only the beginning. You must cultivate your facility, learn the tricks of the trade, and every trade has them, you must practise and work hard. If you are to achieve at least a reasonable standard you must learn to discard that which you know in your heart and soul is not good enough. Alexander Pope said:

'I believe no one qualification is so likely to make a good writer as the power of rejecting his own thoughts. For what I have published I can only hope to be pardoned; but for what I have burned I deserve to be praised.'

He also said of poets, but it applies equally to writers of prose:

'...a poet no sooner communicates his works ....but it is imagined that he is a vain creature given up to the ambition of fame; when perhaps the poor man is all the while trembling with the fear of being ridiculous.'

When writing, sometimes you think it is going really well, it is almost writing itself, this will make wonderful literature; and when you start to write next day you think that what you write is a lot of rubbish that you would be embarrassed that anyone should see. The truth is that what we write is probably somewhere between these two extremes and for most of us much closer to the latter than the former.

You will, no doubt, have heard of writer's block, when for no apparent reason your ideas dry up and your very capacity to write disappears. It may happen in front of the blank screen when you want to begin writing something new or it may happen in the middle of something you are already writing. The first time this happens you may feel that that's the end of it; it was good while it lasted but it's over. Who did I think I was anyway thinking I could write? Nonsense. Let no such thought enter your head. Above all don't give up but tell yourself that you are in good company; many writers, even some of the great ones, go through periods of writer's block, not much of a consolation but none the less. It may be caused by being too ambitious in what you want to write or the feeling takes over that everything you write is no good or worse. It may be caused by exhaustion, anxiety, a family problem or something of which we are not conscious. Since everything we write, fiction or non-fiction, is filtered through us, our own life experience, it may be that writer's block comes from the fear of some truth about ourselves that is buried deep in our subconscious. Just as we must make ourselves vulnerable if we are to love, so we must make ourselves vulnerable if we are to write. The block may last for weeks or months. Writer's block for the writer of fiction has been described as a condition in which your imaginary friends won't talk to you. It is a condition which also afflicts composers.

Whatever its cause, take time off from writing, keep a notebook with you and write down anything that occurs to you that might be pertinent to writing or to a topic you might write about in future. Alternatively, to be modern, you can speak your thoughts into the recorder of your mobile phone and transcribe them later. Try taking regular physical exercise and if when you try to come back to writing the block hasn't gone away, try setting yourself a discipline. Leave what you have been working on there, and each day for a few minutes or longer simply write anything; a line, a paragraph, a page of what you did yesterday, a telephone conversation you had recently, a holiday you would like to plan, what your grandmother once said to you about the world. Write anything for a few minutes or as long as it takes, leave it and get on with your life, but do the same tomorrow. It may take weeks or it may take months, but it will go away and you will be able to write again. There are novels the whole theme of which is writer's block and there is a whole literature on the subject.

Returning to what Pope said, none of us likes to look ridiculous, but go ahead: learn what you can, work hard and follow your instinct. Above all be yourself, don't imitate anybody, don't compare yourself with others, find your own distinctive voice, cultivate your own talent however great or small, and find the wonderful but hard-won satisfaction of writing creatively.

Before I proceed (*à la* the Gardaí) I must declare myself. I may not be as pedantic as my mother was but when writing English, as I have said, I am old fashioned. The likes of me, and there are many of us, are known by modernists in the trade as 'sticklers'. Amongst the cognoscenti there are different opinions on many things concerning the evolution of language and the use of English, so at worst I will give you something from which to dissent. As I have already said, you must make up your own mind, but I suggest that it is better to err on the conservative rather than the liberal side. If you are aware of my prejudices you can then make your own decisions.

Good English is the material of creative writing, and creativity, which is your own individual natural facility cultivated conscientiously, is the tool you use to fashion English into works of art.

Chapter 2. Literary Language

Just because something is published does not mean that it is well written and there are many extremely well written pieces that are never published. The content, the appropriateness to the publisher and the timing can be factors in whether something is published or not. To put it simply, whether something is accepted for publication will finally depend on whether the publisher believes he can sell it. If what you submit to a publisher is poorly or carelessly written, your chances of being published will be diminished and if it is well written, you will not guarantee but improve your chances of success. Furthermore if you expect people to read what you write you owe them the courtesy of writing as well as you can.

Attention to Detail

Attention to detail is important and some of it may seem trivial and of no consequence, but detail is important, so when writing avoid the mistakes commonly made in speech and in writing. With the passage of time some former rules of good writing are going by the board. Those who ignore them justify what they do on the grounds that language is evolving or even that what they say is the important thing and not how they say it. I profoundly disagree with both these excuses for writing poor English. A television interviewer asked Hilary Mantel at the end of an hour long interview: 'Are you happy?' She replied: 'It depends almost entirely on the last sentence I wrote. If it's a good one I'm happy. If I'm plunged into uncertainty about that sentence I have to live with a lot of ambivalence or ambiguity as to whether a scene is going to work.'

Splitting Infinitives

Don't split infinitives (*i.e. Don't split 'to' from the verb by placing an adverb between them*) was considered fifty years ago by strict grammarians to be an unbreakable rule. Today it is is largely ignored.

Although there may no longer be a strict rule on splitting infinitives it remains a useful convention to observe.

'He began to carefully examine the document.' **Not good.**

'He began carefully to examine the document.' **Good.**

'He began to examine the document carefully.' **Good.**

'He began to examine carefully the document.' **OK,** but separates the verb from its object.

'According to the coach it is vital to lock all gates **fully to maintain** the secrecy of training ground moves.' ('Fully' here can refer to 'to lock' instead of to 'to maintain').

'According to the coach it is important to lock all gates **to maintain fully** the secrecy of training ground moves.' ('To maintain fully' separates the verb from its object).

So in this situation it is probably preferable to split the infinitive as follows:

'According to the coach it is vital to lock all gates **to fully maintain** the secrecy of training ground moves.'

Another example of where it may be desirable to split an infinitive: 'she failed completely to understand it'. This is ambiguous; it can mean that she was at a total loss to understand it, or it can mean that she understood it partially. To place 'completely' after the infinitive doesn't help, so to split the infinitive and say 'she failed to completely understand it' if that is what you want to say, may be necessary.

People today for some reason: carelessness, ignorance or simply to be perversely modern, more often than not, choose casually to split infinitives. Or you might prefer 'to casually split'! Again, you must make up your own mind.

Choosing the right option, to keep the infinitive together, is not a matter of keeping a rule for the sake of it. To do so reads better; it is simply better English.

One of the best known examples of a split infinitive is the catch phrase from *Star Trek:* 'to boldly go.' Students have said to me 'but that is better than 'to go boldly.' Is it? Perhaps it is, there are exceptions to the rule of thumb, but is this one of them simply because of its familiarity? If it were not that it is a catch phrase and one of the most famous quotes ever, would it be thought to be the better option? Perhaps so; perhaps not; you decide. There are exceptions to most rules. Anyway in this case I am reliably informed that 'to boldly go' is a piece of dialogue and not narrative. You can put anything you like in dialogue provided it is consistent with the character of the speaker. In writing it is important to know the rule and if you decide to break it, it is important to have good reason for doing so, as with 'to fully maintain' above.

Fowler in his *Dictionary of Modern English Usage* says;

A real split infinitive, though not desirable in itself, is preferable to either of two things; to real ambiguity, and to patent artificiality.

Martin Amis has said that he thinks that to split an infinitive is perfectly legitimate, but that he does his best never to split one in public and that he would certainly not advise anybody else to do so, even today.

In this as in most of the matters to which I give rise, you must decide for yourself.

Ending a Sentence with a Preposition

Another former rule of thumb that is largely ignored today is: **don't end a sentence with a preposition**. A preposition as the last word of a sentence is sometimes known as a dangling preposition.

'He was the boy I gave it to.' **Not good.**

'He was the boy to whom I gave it.' **Good.**

'I gave it to that boy.' **Good.**

'That's the mop I scrubbed the floor with.' **Not good.**

'That's the mop I used to scrub the floor.' **Good.**

With a little thought there is always a way around these things. On the other hand: 'Who is the note on the table for?' is just common sense. To say 'For whom is the note on the table?' would be just foolish. A sentence ending with a preposition like 'to' or 'with' is often weak. To jig around such a sentence so that it ends with a noun or a verb usually makes it stronger. I suspect this is the reason that the rule of thumb became established in the first place and in my opinion it still applies.

There are pedants who want to preserve prescriptive practices of the past, such as not splitting infinitives or not ending sentences with prepositions, for their own sake; the ones that modernists call 'sticklers'. There are also people who take the opposite point of view who believe that to eschew such practices marks them as modern and progressive. I don't wish to be either pedantic or modern and progressive for the sake of it. The reason I believe you ought not to split infinitives or end sentences with prepositions most of the time is simply that not to do so makes, in my opinion, for better English. To quote Coleridge again: *'Is it wise to destroy the wisdom of ages in order to substitute the fancies of a day?'*

Creative writing is an artistic skill, not simply an application of rules for their own sake.

The Infinitive is Preferable to the Participle

'He was late and began to run' is preferable to 'He was late and began running.' Be cautious of your use of the '...ing' words; sometimes they're weak and don't enhance what you want to say.

And and But

'And' and **'but'** are conjunctions and are used to join two sentences. Today it has become a fashion that seems to be acceptable to use them to begin a sentence. I haven't yet seen 'And' as the first word that improved the sentence that followed. Try it if you come across it; make the full stop a comma followed by 'and' and see what you think or omit 'And' and make the first letter of the next word a capital and a new sentence. In my opinion to do either of these improves the impact of the sentence. Much the same principle applies to 'But' when it is used as the first word of a sentence. But then I'm old fashioned, or rather: Then I'm old fashioned! Language evolves but not always for the best. It's not a case of doing something because it has always been done. It is a case of judging the alternatives each on its merits. As a principle you must decide for yourself. I hope you are in no doubt that I have decided for me.

Tautologies

'A new initiative' is a tautology. It is **'an initiative'** unless a previous initiative has been mentioned to which you want to relate it – another initiative.

Me and I

'*John and me,*' or '*me and John*' made the arrangement' are wrong on two counts. "**'John and I'** made the arrangement" is correct. You always put yourself last and check by saying 'John made the arrangement' and 'me made the arrangement' is obviously wrong. Similarly '*He gave it to John and I*' is wrong; check 'He gave it to John' and 'He gave it to I.' **'He gave it to John and me'**.

Common Mistakes in Speech

Common mistakes in speech should not be written: *we done* and *we seen* should be **'we did'** and **'we saw'**. I heard a weather forecast man on TV say '....as you have saw'. I suspect that so careful was he not to say 'seen' that he didn't use it when he should have! *We should have went'* should be **'we should have gone.'** I once heard a Wicklow school headmaster in the course of a short radio interview say 'I done' twice.

You can hear fifty times a day on radio *'there is'* or *'there's'* when it should be **'there are.'** *There is* or *there's* is right when the predicate is singular: **'there is'** or **'there's a horse in that field,'** but **'There are horses in that field'** not *there's horses in that field.* In speech it looks as though this is a case of language evolving but if you think all of this is very pedantic and trivial when writing creatively have another think. If a publisher reads these things in something you submit he is likely to read no further and to throw your manuscript into his capacious tea-chest of rejects because it will cost him time and therefore money to correct your bad English. That is, of course, unless your content is a work of genius.

Here are some more:

I illustrate two important points with the following sentences.

'In 1935 The Barrow Milling Company was opened by Dr Cullen, Bishop of Kildare and Leighlin assisted by five other priests.' **Not good**

Active/Passive Voice

Point 1: Don't use the passive voice if you can use the active, in this case use the active 'opened' not the passive 'was opened by.'

Main Point of Sentence Last

Point 2: The main point of the sentence should be at the end; '…opened the Barrow Milling Company.'

'In 1935 Dr Cullen, Bishop of Kildare and Leighlin, assisted by five other priests, opened the Barrow Milling Company.'

'The RNLI Howth Lifeboat station was donated the proceeds of a boat angling event held last week in Dublin Bay.' ('Irish Times' August 1, 2011.) **Not good**

How about: **'The proceeds of a boat angling event held last week in Dublin Bay were donated to the RNLI Howth Lifeboat Station.'** It is correct to keep the passive 'were donated' here unless you say who donated it, when it would be: **'Local anglers donated the proceeds of a boat angling event held last week to the RNLI Howth Lifeboat Station.' Good**

'It was an emotional occasion for me.' Better; **'it was for me an emotional occasion.'** The main point of the sentence is at the end.

Position of Only

When you use 'only' be careful where you position it. It should be placed as closely as possible to the word to which it refers.

He **only** knew of two houses that had ponds in their gardens. **Wrong.**

He knew of **only** two houses that had ponds in their gardens. **Right.**

Less and Fewer.

There were **less** people at the meeting this week than last week. **Wrong.**

There were **fewer** people at the meeting this week than last week. **Right.**

'Less' for quantity; (there was less corn in the shed..') **'fewer' for number.**

Ugly Words

If possible avoid the use of ugly words and the prince of ugly words is 'got'. It is one of the most over-used words in the language as demonstrated by a Dr Withers, a mid-Victorian writer. He wrote this to make the point:

I got on horseback within ten minutes after I got your letter. When I got to Canterbury I got a chaise for town; but I got wet through, and have got such a cold that I shall not get rid of it in a hurry. I got to the Treasury about noon, but first of all got shaved and dressed. I soon got into the secret of getting a statement before the Board, but I could not get an answer then; however, I got intelligence from a messenger that I should get one next morning. As soon as I got back to my inn I got my supper, and then got to bed. When I got up next morning, I got my breakfast, and, having got dressed, I got out in time to get an answer to my submission. As soon as I got it, I got into a chaise, and got back to Canterbury by three, and got home for tea. I have got nothing further for you, and so adieu.

I have re-written the piece without using the word once.

I mounted my horse within ten minutes of receiving your letter. When I arrived in Canterbury I took a chaise for town, but I was wet through and have such a cold that I shall not shake it off in a hurry. I arrived at the Treasury about noon, but first of all I shaved and dressed. I soon discovered the secret of having a statement accepted by the Board, but no answer was forthcoming then; I had intelligence from a messenger that I should have one next morning. As soon as I arrived back to my inn I had my supper and went to bed. Next morning I had my breakfast and having dressed I left in time to await an answer to my submission. As soon as I received it I took a chaise and arrived back to Canterbury by three, and was home for tea. I have nothing further for you, and so adieu.

Obviously this example is overstated but you can see how, with a little effort, it is easy to avoid poor English.

Avoid use of words like 'nice,' rather say what it was that was nice. Avoid use of 'very' where possible; either omit it or say why it was 'very,' without using the word itself.

Use of Off

The only thing you take **'off'** people are clothes. You take, receive or buy everything else **'from'** somebody.

I took the box of matches **from** my little brother.

I get the magazine **from** a fellow at work.

I bought it **from** a man at the door.

The use of 'off' is so common these days that I think I may be on a loser here, none the less 'from' is preferable.

Comparing

Comparing two things use the comparative, the **'...er'** word.

Comparing more than two things use the superlative, the **'...est'** word.

'Which of these, the pink or the green, is **better?**', not 'best'.

'Which of these three colours is **best?**', not 'better'.

Facts and Detail

Joseph O'Connor in his short story *The Playboy of Glenageary* mentions passing 'St Paul's, Church of Ireland.' This is simply wrong. It should be **'St Paul's Church of Ireland church.'** This mistake is common in newspapers when they refer to the venue of funerals. The 'Church of Ireland' is a national institution and it is incorrect to refer to an individual church building as such. O'Connor's mistake is the equivalent of saying somebody passed *St Mary's Roman Catholic*, rather than **'St Mary's Roman Catholic church'** or someone passed *Aughrim GAA*, rather than **Aughrim GAA Park.**

The point is to pay careful attention to detail, no matter how small, and research carefully when possible rather than rely on memory.

Rare, Posh and Long Words

Don't use rare, posh or long words gratuitously. Only use them if they are necessary. They can attract the attention of the reader and interrupt the flow of the passage. Always use the short word rather than the long word, for example don't use 'calumnious' rather use 'untrue' or 'false'.

In passing, there is no evidence for the popular belief that the etymology of 'posh' is '**P**ort **O**ut **S**tarboard **H**ome', the most desirable position of cabins in the shade when sailing to and from the east in colonial days before air conditioning.

Neither is there any evidence that the etymology of 'snob' is **S**ine **Nob**iltate, the Latin of without nobility. The etymology of both of these words is unknown; an example of what people don't know they often invent, especially if it sounds clever.

I think 'egregious', meaning 'outrageous' or 'notorious', is a delightful word. It comes from the Latin: *grex, gregis* – a flock, and so, 'out of the flock'. It goes beautifully with 'eejit' and so to have somebody called 'you egregious eejit' in dialogue would be a wonderful combination. It could be something that only an old fashioned schoolmaster would call a boy. I would love to have the opportunity to use it in the right context.

Don't use business letter or civil service phrases like 'in due course', 'acknowledge receipt', 'for your perusal'.

Don't use jargon words and phrases, especially those beloved of sports reporters or political journalists. Somebody has said that the collective word for sports journalists is 'a cliché' of sports journalists. The same word could be used of political journalists.

Turn specialist phrases and words, for example scientific words, into ordinary English where possible.

Americanisms

You could make a life study of the differences between English and American English. We forget that many words that are now standard in English English were once Americanisms – 'placate', 'transpire', 'antagonise' and many more. As we have seen language evolves. It seems to me that the criterion in literary English as to whether we use a word or not is primarily whether it says precisely what we want to say and secondly is it euphonious? (I dropped that in just for fun, to make the point in passing that I made above, that you shouldn't use the unusual or big word when you can say the same thing in a simpler way!) ... does it sound well? For example don't use the American 'hike', use the English 'rise'. Which sounds better to your ear? 'A hike in interest rates' or 'A rise in interest rates.' For me, no contest. If the American word sounds better then, all other things being equal, perhaps you should select it. The following two, however, are a bridge too far:

'Bob died on Friday, he will be funeralized on Tuesday.' 'I'm looking for Bill, I need to conversate with him'; the gratuitous turning of nouns into verbs. Use your discretion but don't become a bigot.

Recently, I understand thanks to *Downton Abby, Doctor Who, Harry Potter,* and *Top Gear,* there are signs that the Americans are turning back to their mother tongue!

See www.britishisms.wordpress.com

Long Sentences

Don't use long convoluted sentences with a number of relative clauses. **Break a long sentence into smaller sentences**. For example: 'He lived in a cottage on the side of the road just beyond the creamery where a fleet of carts carrying churns and drawn by a motley crew of donkeys, jennets, ponies and horses arrived every morning and where their owners exchanged the recent news, gossip and scandal of the village to the praise of few and the defamation of many.' **Rather:** 'He lived in a cottage on the side of the road, just beyond the creamery. A fleet of carts carrying churns and drawn by a motley crew of donkeys, jennets, ponies and horses arrived there every morning. Their owners exchanged the recent news, gossip and scandal of the village to the praise of few and the defamation of many.' Be careful of the use of conjunctions as in this case, **'where'** and **'and',** they can lead you into sentences that are too long.

Short Sentences

'At the time sexism was rampant. Women were not invited to the dinner. It was an all male affair.' Short sentences have a strong impact, but this is lost if they are overused. Perhaps this might be better as one sentence: 'Since at the time sexism was rampant, women were not invited to the dinner and so it was an all male affair.' It depends on the context and you must decide. It is a good principle to use both long and short sentences to achieve your effect.

Unnecessary Words

'He said he would like to go back to Africa again.' Omit either 'back' or 'again': 'He said he would like to go to Africa again,' or 'He said he would like to go back to Africa.' Which of these you use may depend on the context; for example, whether his return to Africa is to visit or to live.

Nouns and Verbs

Avoid turning nouns into verbs: noun 'evidence' becoming verb 'evidencing.'

Avoid turning intransitive verbs into transitive verbs: 'progress' intransitive verb being used transitively: 'We hope to progress the enquiry.' Try 'advance'.

If you want to pursue these two large subjects google (itself a verb from a proper noun) 'nouns into verbs' and 'transitive and intransitive verbs,' but don't forget to come back!

Alliteration

Most often illustrated by 'round the rugged rock the ragged rascal ran.' Alliterations can sometimes present themselves to you spontaneously. Too long an alliteration can be a bit too clever. 'He put a perfect proportion of the priceless pepper into the pot'.

Perhaps break the alliteration with 'valuable' for 'priceless'? Maybe not?

*'A **poc**marked enamel sign with a lovingly **p**ainted hand indicated a cement **bloc**house set at a **d**iscreet **d**istance **d**own the **p**latform.'*

('The Book of Evidence,' John Banville.)

A separated '**p**' alliteration, a together '**d**' alliteration and 'block' echoing 'pock..'.

*'…a **m**ysterious **m**iddle-aged couple came, who **s**poke to no one, and grimly walked their **s**ausage dog in **s**ilence at the **s**ame time every **m**orning down **S**tation Road to the **s**trand.'*

('The Sea,' John Banville.)

'm' and 's'; six 'ss' broken by interposing an 'm' that resonates with the two 'ms' at the beginning of the sentence.

Word Selection and Order

When talking about long and short sentences above, why 'news, gossip and scandal' in that order? Why not 'news, scandal and gossip' or 'scandal, gossip and news?' Largely you learn to use the sequence that flows best in the reading and in this case there is also the matter of gradation: news; respectable, gossip; less respectable and scandal; not at all respectable.

Why in Wordsworth's sonnet *Upon Westminster Bridge* did he use the order: '..ships, towers, domes, theatres and temples …'? again the flow of language and he uses 'temples' rather than 'churches' I assume because 'churches' is a word in which the 'ch' sound occurring twice stops the flow. Did he use 'domes' to break the 't' alliteration?

Tennyson in his poem 'To Virgil' says of Virgil's work: 'All the chosen coin of fancy flashing out from many a golden phrase,' and: 'All the charm of all the muses often flowering in a lonely word.'

'In planning the furniture he tried to ensure the optimum level of convenience and comfort.' Or is '.. comfort and convenience' better? Does your choice depend on the context?

Which word selection would you use in the following?

'The house was one of the finest on the most prestigious road in the city's most desirable suburb,' OR

'It was one of the finest houses on the most desirable road in the city's most prestigious suburb.' 'Prestigious' is not a very pleasant word, is there a suitable synonym?

Chiming

Avoid repeating a word in close proximity to the same word used earlier.

'People who do **essential** jobs are often taken for granted, and remember when you need a doctor it is **essential** to make an appointment.' **Not good**.

Even James Joyce was not exempt: see *The Dead* towards the end when Gabriel and Gretta arrive at the hotel:

'An old man was dozing in a great hooded chair in the hall. He lit a candle in the office and went before them to the **stairs.** *They followed him in*

silence, their feet falling in soft thuds on the thickly carpeted **stairs.** *She mounted the* **stairs** *behind the porter.'*

He could have used **'steps'** for the second **'stairs'.** A well known Joycean scholar, who once ran for President of Ireland, to whom I spoke about this told me Joyce knew what he was doing, that he would chime in order to give emphasis. I cannot see what emphasis he would want to make by chiming 'stairs' here. If you're a genius you can get away with murder. Despite feeling nervous criticising James Joyce, I'm sticking to my guns.

Bad Habits

We are all in danger of developing bad habits. Two of mine are overuse of the word 'however' and the phrase 'to say the least.' Watch out for your own.

What I have talked about in this chapter is by no means an exact science. Much of it comes from instinct. Your ear plays a large part, but it is important to be sensitive to all these issues if you are to write well and to this end it is a help to read good English by established writers.

As an exercise read over the following passage a few times and then write the substance of it in your own words.

"To sit still and contemplate, to remember the faces of women without desire, to be pleased by the great deeds of men without envy, to be everything and everywhere in sympathy, and yet content to remain where and what you are. Is not this to know both wisdom and virtue and to dwell with happiness?" (From *'Walking Tours,'* Robert Louis Stevenson.)

Show Don't Tell

This is the best known and most valuable piece of advice for writers. It applies primarily to fiction, but in non-fiction writing it can have application too.

Show the character and reveal the plot by using thoughts, words, feelings and actions rather than by statement or exposition. Showing creates pictures in the reader's mind that are his or her contribution to the story and add pleasure to their experience of reading.

'Show don't tell' is not an absolute. Sometimes the narrator needs to 'tell' in order to move the story on, or to give a break from 'showing'. If showing only is used the writing can become artificial and stilted. A balance is needed. Critical passages should certainly be shown rather than told.

To 'show' use the five senses, action and dialogue.

Tell: 'She arrived home drunk.'

Show: 'She arrived home dishevelled, her eyes were glazed and she slurred her words.'

Tell: 'When she entered his office, she found him dead at his desk.'

Show: 'When she entered his office, he was slumped forward on his desk. She spoke to him. He did not reply. She shook him and could find no pulse.'

Tell: 'Kathleen was boring.'

Show: 'Kathleen recounted how she had coped with a similar problem and expressed in great detail her opinion on this as she did on every other topic under the sun.'

Tell: 'He smashed the bottle;'

Show: 'He banged the bottle against the table and scattered shards of glass across the room.'

'Don't **tell** me the moon is shining; **show** me the glint of light on broken glass.' **Anton Chekhov**

Style

Style is difficult to define. It is to do with language and is not appraised by our intellects, but by our emotions. We feel style. Style is a quality possessed in a greater or lesser degree, or perhaps not possessed at all.

Words through their content convey **meaning to our intellects**. They also convey, through the sound of the words, their order and everything else about them, **something to our sensibilities**. These two together constitute style. How do we effect this co-ordination? By choice of words.

I have already dealt with some aspects of word choice. Here are some further important matters that will influence style:

Onomatopoeic Words

'Whisper,' 'rush,' 'rattle,' 'crackle,' 'mud,' 'tremulous,' sound just like what they mean. Use them sparingly, but when you do, their sound adds to their meaning.

Words of Association

Words that evoke feelings and memories, e.g. home, mother, childhood, friends and dentist! These words have meaning in the immediate context but often add subconscious associations of the past, either positive or negative.

The Pattern of Letters

We have already alluded to this. Here is an explicit example:

'The great wheel began to move and went quicker and quicker until you couldn't see the spokes.'

The 'k' sounds are inimical to the smooth process of a big wheel getting faster. What about:

'The great wheel began to turn, it built up speed slowly until it spun so fast that nothing was visible between the hub and the rim.'

The choice and pattern of words should reflect the content of the sentence.

Style is intuitive. It is writing with sensibility and sensitivity. There is no rulebook. It is to do with the heart and the ear of the individual, and the blending of the intellect and the emotions. Some by nature will have a greater ability to write with style than others. It cannot be forced, but awareness of it may help any of us to develop our capacity for it. Content is what is immediate to a reader and for many is solely that by which they judge what they read. However the reader with aesthetic awareness will appreciate the style. On the other hand, I once listened to an author read his piece of non-fiction on radio. I was appreciating the beauty and style of his language so much that I realised I wasn't listening to the content. When reading *Émile*, Kant was alert to the seductive dangers of Rousseau's language; he worried that its beauty detracted from his ideas.

Four Methods in the Art of Literature.

Exposition, Argumentation, Narration and Description.

Exposition

Is exposing or laying out something. It is explaining. It is from intellect to intellect and has least need of style. Exposition can be an interruption to the flow of the story.

Argumentation

More amenable to style since it is important to convince the reader's emotions and intellect.

Narration and Description

In these there is full scope for the sound of the language used to play upon the reader's sensibilities, while the content is speaking to his intellect.

Above all, and I cannot emphasise this too strongly, **do not get hung up on all of these dos and don'ts so that you become inhibited when you are writing**. You must not be intimidated by them. Everybody gets things wrong from time to time. As you have seen even top-class writers get them wrong, for example Joseph O'Connor and, unless I am missing something, James Joyce; both as quoted above. Don't let concern for the dos and don'ts inhibit your flow of inspiration. Get down on paper what it is you want to say and you can pick up as many of these things as you can spot in subsequent drafts. Your later drafts are to edit the work, polish layout, grammar, syntax and all the things we have been talking about. Read and re-read leaving time between so that on each occasion you return to it you see it afresh. Raymond Carver, the American writer when referring to Evan Connell another writer said that he knew he was finished with a short story when he found himself going through it and taking out commas and then going through the story again and putting commas back in the same places. He liked that way of working on something and respected that kind of care for what is being done.

This kind of fine tuning is important so that your finished work is the best you can do. You are unlikely to get everything right. I have no doubt that somewhere in this work I have fallen into one or more of the faults that I have warned against!

A great literary name doesn't guarantee perfection. All of the great writers had their limitations. **Cervantes' *Don Quixote*** is one of the greatest novels ever written. It is criticised by the cognoscenti for aspects of its structure. **Scott in his Waverley novels** is said to be short on style. **Guy de Maupassant,** though his stories are wonderful to read said nothing of significance to the world. It should be an encouragement to us that none of the great is without fault of one kind or another. The aphorism: 'Comparisons are odorous' is nowhere more applicable than in the field of creative writing. Don't compare yourself to others, great or small. Be your own person, do it your own way, never imitate. Say what it is you want to say to the best of your ability and what you write will be authentic, and above all enjoy it. You cannot do better than that.

CHAPTER 3. LITERARY FORMS

Creative Non-Fiction

Creative non-fiction is the writing of true and accurate accounts of real people, places and events using literary language. It doesn't simply deal in bare facts. It expresses the truth in a creative way, remaining factually accurate but using literary techniques to make the writing interesting. It has been described as 'reality presented with style'.

When you write creative non-fiction your unique voice presents the facts in such a way as to arrest the interest of the reader. Two pointers for writing short pieces of creative non-fiction are: don't make your beginning obvious. Start somewhere else, as it were, from where you lead into your main theme. Alastair Cook in his *Letter from America* was a master of this. Secondly, look for the landing lights, in other words keep constantly before you your planned dénouement. You arrest and keep the interest of your reader if you employ an unlikely slant on your subject and introduce an element of surprise. You make the facts come alive through your narration. It is a genre where it is particularly important to show rather than tell. You never fabricate or alter facts or events. You write about real people and by your writing you make them live for the reader.

Some would say starkly that there is no such thing as non-fiction. By this they mean that the real people and events of the past have gone. The Greek philosopher Heraclitus famously said that you can't step into the same river twice. Even if we have witnessed the events that we recount, whether recent or distant, it is inevitable that we filter them through our unique selves, our life experiences and our prejudices and that this filtering will unconsciously influence how we present them. Two people who have witnessed a car crash standing side by side five minutes previously, while agreeing that the event occurred will often give widely different accounts of it. The difference can be attributed to the uniqueness of the two individuals. Our memories are as they are, and furthermore when we research events we may find they differ from our memory of them. We can do no more than the best we are able to present facts with integrity. For example we will have embedded in our memory something somebody said or did twenty or thirty years ago. The precise words or the recall of the event may or may not have altered in our minds in the intervening time, we cannot be certain; our imagination may play a part in altering what we believe we remember accurately. What we remember today may be influenced by occasions when we remembered and recounted the events in the intervening years and perhaps the response of those to whom we recounted them. As we remember past events we remember in vignettes. Joseph Conrad said:

'The effect of perspective in memory is to make things loom large because the essentials stand out isolated from their surrounding of insignificant daily facts which have naturally faded out of one's mind.'

We remember in this way what was particularly significant for us at the time. Our memories often fill out these vignettes or episodes to give them context. This filling out, especially of the distant past, may be imaginative and not factually accurate. It may combine memory with other knowledge of events and reassemble them to fit the requirements of the context of the re-telling. Frederic Bartlett, a Cambridge experimental psychologist, believed that memory was a manufactured product designed to give meaning and direction to the present, even at the expense of strict accuracy about the past. A striking finding of Bartlett was the ease and extent to which people unselfconsciously fabricate what they cannot retrieve from previous experience. Other research suggests that the brain doesn't simply store and retrieve memories, it restructures them. Memory is creative, fallible and prone to suggestion and other distorting influences, often to support a case we want to make or to bolster our ego. Fintan O'Toole has said that memory is shaped by politics, by myth, by the demands of narrative by the desire to find some kind of meaning in the absurdity of death.

What is important when writing creative non-fiction is that what we recount is in good faith and is as *far as it is possible* true to the person who is remembered and to what they said or did.

The genre of creative non-fiction includes: biography, memoir, essay, travel writing, food writing, nature writing and some forms of journalism. It is a characteristic of the genre that it allows and even encourages the writer to become part of the story that is being written. The term itself, creative non-fiction, has only been used since the late 1970s to describe writing that is about people and events from the real world in contrast to fiction that is accounts that are fabricated by the writer's mind. It is something of a paradox that some people will say that there is no such thing as non-fiction, and yet fiction, using invented characters, settings and events is about human experiences of the real world!

Two classic examples of creative non-fiction by great writers, both written long before the term was coined, are Robert Louis Stevenson's *Travels with a Donkey in the Cévennes* and George Orwell's *Down and Out in Paris and London*. All of us with an instinct to write have within us to some degree the capacity to write creative non-fiction, in that we have lived to adulthood and have had unique life experiences.

Fiction

Fiction is the truth as we see it about some aspect of the human condition. The action may never have happened but it has happened, in some shape or form, to somebody sometime.

James Plunkett said that you can't manufacture material. A writer never writes a story about a subject. He uses a subject in order to write himself.

Pat Schneider has said that all fiction is autobiography, because even that which we imagine is a collage of images and meanings that have come into, and have been transformed by, our minds. Fiction is *an autobiography of the imagination.* Fiction is another way of telling the truth. It is an oft repeated adage: we do not choose our subject; it chooses us.

The subject we write may very consciously be something from our own life experience, or it may be something from deep down in our subconscious. Whatever it is it must be real for us and we must treat it honestly. You may say 'I don't want to write about myself, I want to write fiction.' You may not want to write factual, chronological information about yourself, but in the sense that experience of life for you is distilled internally you write yourself.

Sometimes our motivation to write comes from some unresolved experience of our early life. If you try to manufacture material it will appear faked and lack conviction, and will make for poor writing. It must come from you and your real life experience. This can be conscious, sub-conscious or even unconscious.

Pat Schneider has said that none of us creates *ex nihilo*. All writing involves self revelation. Even if the actual facts of our lives are not revealed, she maintains that we cannot escape the fact that writing reveals the way our minds work.

J M Coetzee tells us that in a larger sense, all writing is autobiography; everything that you write, including criticism and fiction, writes you as you write it.

The Short Story

Drama and poetry existed in the ancient world. The origin of the novel is widely disputed and depending on the criteria of which literary expert you accept it emerged first in English probably in the eighteenth century. A favourite contender for first novel in the sense in which we understand the novel today, though epistolary in form, was Samuel Richardson's *Pamela*, 1740.

The short story as a genre is generally accepted to have started with the publication of the American writer Nathaniel Hawthorne's book *Twice Told Tales* in 1837. Daniel Defoe wrote the introduction to this work and referred to the contents as 'prose tales.' He famously referred to short stories as 'unified works of fiction that could be read in a single sitting.' In time this criterion for the short story became the three unities, similar to those that French seventeenth century dramatists derived from Aristotle. That is the short story should have **unity of place**: there should be only one setting; **unity of time**: the story should take place within one day; and **unity of action**: there should be one main action with no sub-plots. Of the two great nineteenth century masters of the short story, Guy de Maupassant adhered more to these principles than Chekhov. Both deviated as the short story developed and modern short story writers have moved on, but the best short stories observe the spirit of these principles. It is a good exercise when starting to write short stories to observe the three unities simply as a discipline. It makes for good learning of the craft. Someone has pointed out that according to these criteria, only two of Boccaccio's

100 stories in the *Decameron* are technically short stories and the parable of the prodigal son in the New Testament has some of the essential characteristics of a short story.

It is important if you are to do well in any branch of writing; drama, poetry, the novel or the short story, that you read the masters of each of these. For the short story for example, Guy de Maupassant and Anton Chekhov, Ireland's Frank O'Connor and William Trevor, and the short stories of some of the great novelists.

The short story is fiction. Fiction is a means of telling the truth. Its purpose is to use invented places, characters and action to hold up truths about the human condition and human behaviour. One writer put it: 'The writer of fiction forsakes the realm of fact in order that he may better tell the truth, and lures the reader away from actualities in order to present him with realities. The author first transmutes the **concrete actualities** of life **into abstract realities;** and then he transmutes these abstract realities **into concrete imaginings**. The great characters of fiction are typical of large classes of mankind.'

Unless the characters of fiction act and think at all points consistently with the laws of their imagined existence, and unless these laws are in harmony with the laws of actual life, no amount of sophistication on the part of the author can make us finally believe his story; and unless we believe his story, his purpose in writing it will have failed.

Any honest writer will tell you that his characters often stubbornly refuse at certain points to accept the incidents which he has planned for them, and that at other times they take matters into their own hands and can run away with the story. The laws of life, and not the author's will, must finally decide the destinies of heroes and of heroines.

Robert Louis Stevenson once remarked that whenever, in a story by a friend of his, he came upon a passage that was notably untrue, he always suspected that it had been transcribed directly from actual life. 'Oh, no, it's true! It happened to a friend of mine!' However, an actual occurrence is not necessarily true in the context of fiction. The writer needs to find the principle behind the actual occurrence and then employ that principle credibly and true to the characters of the work of fiction.

Point of View

When you sit down to write a short story you must decide **point of view**. Where does the narrator stand in relation to the character and events of the story? Two options: **First Person** (person speaking) **or Third person** (spoken about). Second person, (spoken to), sometimes called 'apostrophe', is less usual.

Objective Point of View

Where the narrator is like an unseen witness. If so you give the facts only, but cannot know thoughts and feelings of characters. You are close to the characters, but never in their heads. Using this point of view it can be hard to keep the reader's interest.

Omniscient Point of View

The narrator knows all and can reveal the thoughts, feelings and actions of all the characters.

Shifting Person Point of View

There are different possibilities of moving between first and third person and changing narration between characters within the story or outside it.

For beginners it is wisest to stick to either **omniscient third person** or **first person.** First person limits the narrator to recounting his own thoughts and feelings.

There are three elements to a short story, **setting, character and action.** Short stories usually have an emphasis on one of these. Short means that you have few characters, few events, and a narrow compass of time and place. The story has four essential ingredients, **character, conflict, crisis and change.**

Setting

Use the senses to make the setting real. It is not always necessary to over-describe or to delineate it all at once. It is sometimes better to thread it through the story as it becomes necessary or appropriate. One landscape many scenes. Setting is not just the physical setting of the room, the house or the countryside, the setting is context; commerce, sport or religion.

Characters

The reader must be able to identify or believe in the characters. The chief character should be unusual, out of the ordinary, have an unlikely characteristic or a problem. He should engage the curiosity of the reader. He may be in pursuit of something, be in a crux or a dilemma and be somehow constrained in his freedom by his personality or circumstance. For the short story one main, two subsidiary characters and perhaps a walk-on character or two are plenty. You have failed if the reader has to go back to remind himself who one of the characters is and where he fits in. Use only those aspects of the characters that are necessary for the story. Characters should be worth knowing. They should be more worth our while than the average actual person, more significant of elements of human nature. One writer tells us that they are quintessential of a type and yet individual with certain traits that distinguish them from representatives of their class. They may be on the margins, but believable. In a short story there is no time to develop character, so they must be described quickly and clearly.

Conflict/Crisis

The problem or dilemma of the main character leads to conflict which in turn leads to some kind of crisis. This is what holds the reader. A story of a respectable, predictable, successful character without conflict or crisis will flop. You can't make a short story out of a suited accountant with a prospering practice, a successful marriage, two wonderful children, one of each, who lives in an affluent suburb, plays golf once a week and goes to church on Sunday. That is, of course, unless he is having a torrid affair with an Estonian office cleaner who has hacked into his firm's computer system and is embezzling vast sums of money that she is sending home to fund the setting up of a chain of brothels, in which case you write the story about the office cleaner. On the way to crisis, partial disclosure creates suspense, but if you give away too much too soon the story is undermined. The ultimate is to achieve a climax to your story within which another unexpected crisis emerges – the crisis within a crisis, the element of surprise.

Change

The ending should show rather than tell briefly what has changed since the beginning of the story as the result of the crisis. The situation at the end of the story must be significantly different from the way it was at the outset.

Plot

The plot in a novel is the weaving together of more than one strand. In the short story the plot is a single strand or an arc out of the circle of the life of the main character; a slice of life. Every word you write must count and be related to the plot; no unnecessary words: 'The phone rang. A woman's voice at the other end asked......' No need to say 'He answered it.' A writer must be ruthless in what to put in and especially in what to leave out. The adage is 'if in doubt leave it out.' It is almost always the case that a writer who must reduce the number of words of a previously completed story for entry to a competition or for publication, in doing so finds that reducing the word count improves the story. The best short stories are built before they are written. You need to have your outline plot worked out before you start but not your detail and incidents. However, as I have said, as the plot develops interesting things can sometimes happen that the writer hadn't planned.

A plot needs a beginning, a middle and an end for it to work. Plot is the result of choices made by characters. Keep the reader guessing, but hold the solution until the end. Don't leave the dénouement to one sentence at the very end. As I have said, the end must indicate that as a result of the events a permanent change has taken place. Leave the reader to draw natural and obvious conclusions; don't spell everything out. It adds to the enjoyment of the reader if he makes the deductions. Sometimes it is enough simply to mention things. In fact, sometimes it can be enough simply to *imply* or hint at them. On the other hand don't make jumps the reader cannot make. Language used must be in tune with the mood of the story. For example in a story about deception or betrayal use words like 'wicked,' 'unconscionable,' 'anger,' and avoid words like 'gentle,' 'harmony,' relaxed.'

The Title

Usually no more than two or three words that say something about the story and may even add something to it that will save narrative or exposition in the story itself.

The Opening Sentence

The opening sentence should invoke a strong sensation that resonates immediately with the reader. It often makes the best impact if it is short; 'Mrs Mooney was a butcher's daughter.' (*The Boarding House*, James Joyce). 'I could never understand all the old talk about how hard it is to be a saint.' (*The Face of Evil*, Frank O'Connor). 'Like all children, I led a double life.' (*The Death of Peggy Meehan*, William Trevor). You may want to change your opening sentence well into the story or even at the end, in order to improve it.

It helps if you can begin a short story of setting with a description: 'The office was an unhappy place to work.' A story of character should start with a remark about the leading character: 'My uncle was not to be trusted.' A short story of action should start with a sentence of action: 'The explosion blew the roof off the little house.'

Emphasis of Language

Emphasis of language is particularly important in the short story. If you say 'he strode,' he 'crept' or he 'skulked' down the road, you are saying much more in one word than saying 'he went'.

Clarity

Use an easy-to-envisage setting and make the crisis or climax easily understood. Avoid complexity.

Dialogue

Use of dialogue is a useful way to reveal character. It can suggest a subtlety of character to which the reader is left to tumble. It is also a useful device to break up long passages of narrative and it is used to forward the plot. Much of the time in dialogue it is obvious who the speaker is from what he says. Use 'he said,' 'she said,' known as 'tags' or 'ascription,' only if necessary. In his short story *A Clean Lighted Place* Ernest Hemingway uses tags so sparingly in long sequences of dialogue that it is hard to tell in places who is talking. How a character says something should be clear from what he or she has to say rather than using 'he fumed,' or 'he barked'. Use adverbs in tag lines only rarely: 'he said *politely* or 'she said *coyly.*' The politeness or the coyness should be shown in what the character says and the way that he or she says it.

The Senses

Smell, taste, sight, sound and feel; use them to create atmosphere and enhance the dialogue.

Metaphor and Simile

Use, but do not overuse them. Don't use the ones everybody does; make up your own.

Avoid clichés or invent your own! Steer clear of well-worn plots unless you can produce a new twist, for example, mistaken identity, thwarting inheritance, fake jewels. The last one was used twice by de Maupassant in *The Necklace* and *The Jewels*. These plots have been 'done' by the masters and many times since.

Length

How short is short? It is the greatest economy of words necessary to the story. H.H.Munro (Saki) wrote some stories of less than 1,000 words, while Chekhov wrote short stories of 10,000 – 12,000 words. Some consider *Heart of Darkness*, a notable work of English literature of 39,000 words by Joseph Conrad, to be a short story; many would disagree!

The Novel

Most of the matters we have already looked at in the short story apply equally to the novel, for example the writing, use of language, point of view, use of dialogue, and working towards a crisis or climax. There are, however, important differences between the novel and the short story. They are primarily to do with the plot and characters. In the short story the plot is single and simple. In the novel there is a main plot that develops as the work progresses and is interwoven with sub-plots to make the story. In the short story there is one crisis. In the novel there is room for mini-crises on the way. In the short story there is room for only a limited number of characters and then only a slice of their lives. The novel allows for a number of characters and, for what is particularly important and necessary, the development of character. The short story uses only a limited setting while the novel can roam further abroad. Somebody has said: 'The short story is a focus on one aspect. The novel is life in the round.'

To write a novel is to show a series of scenes, each leading to the next, during which the characters are developed and drive the plot towards the climax. Firstly the author introduces the characters, establishes the setting and outlines the conflict that at the climax must be resolved one way or another. This process must not reveal too much of the characters too quickly, or the likely outcome of the plot, but must raise the interest and curiosity of the reader as soon as possible. This torments those appalling people who having started to read, skip to the end of the book early on to discover the dénouement and then go back and read the rest of the novel.

The middle portion of the story should include events that lead towards the resolution of the conflict and reveal more about the characters. How often have you read a novel that drags in the middle before picking up again towards the end? You must try to avoid this dragging during which not much appears to be happening to hold the interest of the reader who is eager at this point to learn of the resolution; the reader is saying in his head to the author: 'Get on with it.' This dull middle period happens to even the most competent novelists.

The climax resolves the conflict and must do so in such a way as to satisfy the anticipation of the reader. It answers the questions that the writer has given rise to by the interaction of the characters during the story. Just as with the short story the ultimate is to have a climax within a climax and if possible followed by an apparent resolution leading to the actual resolution. If you can, send the reader down a wrong but credible track and then surprise him with your equally credible solution.

Choices that the characters make drive the plot forward and these choices should be believable and consistent with the character. Along the way minor crises create tension and expectation to hold the attention of the reader. It is impossible to keep a story at the height of tension and interest all of the time. What goes up must come down; when there are ups of tension and expectation, by definition they must be followed by downs and the author must make these downs as interesting as possible. Using humour, if it is appropriate, is one way of doing this. However there is nothing worse than humour for its own sake dragged by the neck into a story.

Before you start it can be useful to draft a brief outline of the story with the various movements and developments. This can include listing the main characters with their essential characteristics and how these develop. It can be particularly useful to draw a sketch map of scenes and settings to be sure your locations are all possible and relate to each other credibly.

As a check list ask yourself:

- Does your opening capture immediately the interest of the reader or is it dull and rambling?

- Does the ending of each chapter heighten the expectation of the next?

- Does one chapter lead logically to the next and with each one does the story move forward?

- Is the tension or interest in the story developing throughout?

- Are all the developments of the characters relevant to the story?

- Have you used any sub-plots or digressions that are not pertinent to the main thrust of the story? If so get rid of them or make them pertinent.

In Conclusion

In most things we learn to do, like driving a car, baking a cake or mixing cement, when we begin we must consciously learn and remember and apply the principles and techniques. As time passes the method becomes part of us so that we can talk to a passenger, answer the children's questions or talk to a neighbour while we get on with the task. To some extent this is the case with the principles and techniques of writing that I have outlined. However, it's not quite the same. No matter how careful you are as you write you will get some things wrong and it is one of the purposes of drafting and re-drafting to pick up our mistakes. As I have already said I have no doubt that despite many drafts of this work you will find violations of the principles that I have espoused in it!

That's it. If you get as much satisfaction from writing as I have done, despite the disappointments, you will have a wonderful time. Good luck. It is hard work. It can be lonely but it is very fulfilling. Enjoy it.

ABOUT THE AUTHOR

Patrick Semple is a former Church of Ireland clergyman. Patrick has had two volumes of memoirs published, and two collections of poems. He was editor of 'A Parish Adult Education Handbook,' and ghost wrote 'That Could Never Be,' a memoir by Kevin Dalton. He has had short stories published and broadcast. His novel 'Transient Beings' and his travelogue 'Curious Cargo: Voyages to the West Indies, South and Central America and the Mediterranean' were both published in 2012.

Patrick teaches a creative writing course at the National University of Ireland Maynooth, Adult Education Department and for the last three years has done public readings of his work in Kempten, Bavaria.

He has a website at *www.patricksemple.ie*

CURIOUS CARGO
A travelogue by Patrick Semple

Imagine standing under the stars at sea and wondering at Man's place in the universe with a fellow traveller who can draw on Voltaire, Joyce and the classics. Gentle but tenacious, Patrick Semple is aware of the human frailty that drives the machine.

This is an account of voyages taken by Patrick and his wife Hilary on cargo vessels carrying everything from bananas to buses. They are the sort of people you love to bump into in foreign parts. Self reliant but willing to share, private but willing to open up, self effacing but full of resources and nuggets of survival gold.

This is the kind of travelling the world thinks has passed into folklore. Midnight coffee on the bridge with the captain; weeks at sea between ports; colour, culture and novelty when you put to shore. There are storms and placid sunlit seas. There is the sound of the ocean and all the while the "machine is machining".

In this mode of travel there is time to reflect and space to set the mind free. Take this voyage and you will never take a banana or a vegetarian for granted again.

TRANSIENT BEINGS

A novel by Patrick Semple

Some transient beings come from the past and pass through the present and some in the present refuse to leave the past. How long will the idyllic rectory in the heart of rural Ireland in the 1970's hide the secrets of those who live behind its walls?

Patrick Semple's writing has been described as having a depth of learning and an earnestness of purpose with a selfless immersion in the lives of the characters in the best traditions of John McGahern and Brian Moore.

Transient Beings is a surprising, intelligent and brave story of addiction and belief. It is also the story of the rector as he struggles to understand his duty, his wife and his place in the world. It is a story from the heart as we follow the rector into a growing nightmare of rationalisation. It gives a voice to those people whose life is religion and who find they are forced to reassess their own beliefs.

'There is no greater heresy than that the office sanctifies the holder of it.' and this is as true for the rector's wife as it is for the rector.

Lightning Source UK Ltd.
Milton Keynes UK
UKOW031108130613

212205UK00008B/200/P